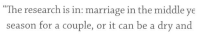

"The research is in: marriage in the middle ye[...] season for a couple, or it can be a dry and [...] the know. We're thankful that Dorothy Littell Greco has provided a life-giving guide for every couple in the second half of marriage, and it is sure to help you flourish. This book is grounded, insightful, and immeasurably practical."

Les and Leslie Parrott, founders of the Center for Relationship Development at Seattle Pacific University, authors of *Saving Your Marriage Before It Starts*

"Impressive and inspirational, the best thing about *Marriage in the Middle* is its hefty bravery. Featuring candid interviews with real couples who've scaled the hard mountains of marital mayhem, Dorothy Greco minces no steps in offering no-nonsense insights on how, with God's help, to survive the unexpected and manage the unmanageable. For those struggling to unravel the tangle of marriage in midlife, she offers truth, practical help and, most of all, hope to outlast the maelstroms while daring to imagine together your brighter days and better ways. A sturdy and inspiring resource."

Patricia Raybon, author of *I Told the Mountain to Move* and *My First White Friend*

"Wise. Honest. Insightful. Helpful. These are just some of the descriptors that emerged as I read Dorothy Greco's *Marriage in the Middle*. With over forty years of marriage racked up myself, I can testify that this book casts a clear and hopeful vision for marriage in the second half of life. Read it and run into the future of your marriage!"

Elisa Morgan, cohost of Discover the Word and president emerita of MOPS International

"In this candid and fearlessly vulnerable book, Dorothy Littell Greco draws from decades of experience guiding married couples as well as from her own thirty-year marriage. Greco's empathetic yet prophetic invitation will inspire couples from every race, tribe, and tongue to contend for their sacred unions. Although we have also been married for almost three decades, *Marriage in the Middle* challenged us to keep moving forward and got us excited about the new adventures in love that lie ahead. We encourage you to listen and learn from this inspiring woman. For those with ears to hear, we believe the Holy Spirit will use this work to speak vision and hope at this stage in your life and marriage."

Sheila Wise Rowe, author of *Healing Racial Trauma*, and **Nicholas Rowe,** vice president for student and global engagement at Gordon College

"I am so grateful for this book and for Dorothy Greco. After forty-two years of marriage, typical marriage books just don't cut it. I need a book and an author who gets the wildly textured ups and downs of long, shared histories, who still can inspire me forward. Greco does this brilliantly. She has woven together an astonishing blend of research, theology, interviews, and personal stories; I am nearly breathless with insight and encouragement. This book will change your marriage."

Leslie Leyland Fields, author of *Your Story Matters: Finding, Writing, and Living the Truth of Your Life*

"The journey of marriage through midlife is demanding and complex. For those navigating this difficult terrain, Greco provides wise, practical, and hopeful counsel. It's like water for the thirsty midlife soul. Three cheers for *Marriage in the Middle!*"

Brad Wong, lead pastor of The River Church Community, San Jose

"Having been married for over three decades, we have learned that long-time love is challenging and that the rewards can be magnificent. In *Marriage in the Middle*, Dorothy Greco offers tested wisdom that rings true to our experience. We heartily recommend it as a good guide for making the lasting, fruitful journey of marriage over a lifetime."

Alan and Gem Fadling, coauthors of *What Does Your Soul Love?* and cofounders of Unhurried Living, Inc.

"The stresses and challenges that come fast and furious at midlife test most marriages and permanently fracture some. Dorothy Greco has a long track record of contending for marriage and is a frank, seasoned guide through the challenging relational terrain of this life stage. Her wonderful *Marriage in the Middle* addresses many topics—including physical and sexual changes, caregiving responsibilities, loss, disappointment, and the reconfiguration of the family—with grace, intelligence, and hope. Greco's insight will help couples love and cherish one another for better, worse, richer, poorer, in sickness and in health for the second half of their journey through life together."

Michelle Van Loon, author of *Becoming Sage: Cultivating Maturity, Purpose, and Spirituality at Midlife*

"My husband, Nathan, and I will soon turn the corner on two decades of married life. Surprisingly, I have more questions now than I did when we first started out together. That's why I'm grateful for the practical wisdom and spiritual insight of Dorothy Greco's *Marriage in the Middle*. With a keen pastoral sensibility, Greco guides readers through the unique challenges—and opportunities!—of marriages that might have a few miles on them. Don't be surprised if, after reading it, you come away with renewed hope and the confidence that the best truly is yet to come."

Hannah Anderson, author of *All That's Good: Recovering the Lost Art of Discernment*

"*Marriage in the Middle* is a fount of wisdom. How refreshing! Greco comes out strong, weaving narrative and research together seamlessly. I found myself nodding my head and rereading so I could digest her insights and hard-won wisdom about midlife and particularly marriage in midlife. Moreover, this book isn't rigid and overly prescriptive—nor does it rely on caricatures of gender roles as so many evangelical books on marriage are wont to do. Greco is nuanced and her insights correspond to the realities of marriage, not some idealistic fantasy of marriage. Read it, put it on your shelf, and recommend it when folks ask you about books on marriage. I certainly will."

Marlena Graves, author of *The Way Up Is Down*

DOROTHY LITTELL GRECO

MARRIAGE IN THE MIDDLE

EMBRACING MIDLIFE SURPRISES, CHALLENGES, AND JOYS

An imprint of InterVarsity Press
Downers Grove, Illinois

InterVarsity Press
P.O. Box 1400, Downers Grove, IL 60515-1426
ivpress.com
email@ivpress.com

InterVarsity Press® is the book-publishing division of InterVarsity Christian Fellowship/USA®, a movement of students and faculty active on campus at hundreds of universities, colleges, and schools of nursing in the United States of America, and a member movement of the International Fellowship of Evangelical Students. For information about local and regional activities, visit intervarsity.org.

Unless otherwise indicated, all Scripture quotations are taken from the Holy Bible, New Living Translation, copyright ©1996, 2004, 2007, 2013. Used by permission of Tyndale House Publishers, Inc., Carol Stream, Illinois 60188. All rights reserved.

Published in association with the literary agency of Credo Communications, LLC, Grand Rapids, MI, www.credocommunications.net.

While any stories in this book are true, some names and identifying information may have been changed to protect the privacy of individuals.

Cover design and image composite: David Fassett
Interior design: Daniel van Loon
Images: wedding rings: © mikroman6 / Moment Collection / Getty Images

ISBN 978-0-8308-4829-4 (print)
ISBN 978-0-8308-5339-7 (digital)

Printed in the United States of America ∞

InterVarsity Press is committed to ecological stewardship and to the conservation of natural resources in all our operations. This book was printed using sustainably sourced paper.

Library of Congress Cataloging-in-Publication Data
A catalog record for this book is available from the Library of Congress.

P 25 24 23 22 21 20 19 18 17 16 15 14 13 12 11 10 9 8 7 6 5 4 3 2 1

Y 36 35 34 33 32 31 30 29 28 27 26 25 24 23 22 21 20

For

Val and Tom

Dan and Kathy

Erik and Jean

Chuck and Marianne

*Thank you for showing us
the beauty and the wonder of marriage in the middle.*

CONTENTS

INTRODUCTION

Congratulations on making it to the middle of life while married. No single narrative could possibly encompass all of our lives. We might be unemployed, launching an encore career, retired, well established in the job of our dreams, or homeschooling young children. Some of us are training for marathons while others are recovering from heart attacks. We might be choosing preschools for our kids, grad schools for ourselves, and assisted living facilities for our parents—all in the same month. Some of us are newlyweds, some are newly remarried, and others are celebrating thirty or even forty years together. And as it pertains to the state of our marriage, we might be hitting our stride or wondering if we're going to make it.

Regardless of where we find ourselves, at least two threads connect us.

First, we're all facing the limits of our power. We cannot slow down the passing of time or stop the effects of aging. We can't influence the stock market or control how our parents' lives will end. These are sobering and often overwhelming realities.

Second, the intense demands and rapidly changing circumstances of midlife force all of us to constantly adjust and adapt. Caregiving responsibilities will decrease in certain areas and increase in others, leaving us off balance and uncertain about what's being asked of us. Seismic shifts in the workplace will force us to be more agile. Spiritual practices that previously helped us to connect with God may begin to feel empty, compelling us to discover new forms of worship.

Yet in the same season, we should begin to experience a sense of satisfaction in all that we've accomplished and a growing clarity about who we are. We may even feel like we could teach a master class on adulting. At least on good days.

None of us will be exempt from the many reverberations of midlife. Ultimately, disequilibrium is a good thing because it forces us out of our comfortable routines and invites us to reinvest in every aspect of our life—including marriage.

⁓

My primary goals for this book are threefold: to articulate the hows and whys of the disequilibrium, to assure you that you're not alone, and to offer both encouragement and strategies that will help you thrive in this season. You'll discover a wealth of relevant, practical information in the coming pages, but you won't find clichés or formulas. Instead, *Marriage in the Middle* will meet you where you are and model vulnerability, promote honesty, and offer grounded hope.

Vulnerability, honesty, and hope are all evident in the interviews that begin and end chapters two through ten. The men and women I spoke with are from diverse ethnic backgrounds, including African American, African Caribbean, Asian, Black, Latina, and Caucasian (these descriptors were chosen by the interviewees). Their words are verbatim, but names and some identifying details have been changed to protect their privacy. My husband, Christopher, also weighs in throughout the book. (He also signed off on everything. Even the painfully honest sections about his family.)

Marriage in the Middle addresses many, but certainly not all, of the issues faced by those of us who are roughly between the ages of forty and sixty-five. Though tomes have been written on trauma and attachment issues, I included a chapter on each, hoping that readers will recognize how these topics may affect their marriages. Questions at the end of each chapter will help you go deeper and serve as conversation starters for couples or small groups.

And if you've read my earlier book, *Making Marriage Beautiful*, please know that *Marriage in the Middle* does not repackage that content. However, you will recognize some thematic overlap—after all, I still follow Jesus and I'm still married to the same man.

⁓⊷⊶

Midlife can often leave us feeling like we're out in the middle of the sea in a tiny boat with a single sail. Though we have little power over the frequency or intensity of the storms that rage around us, we do have tremendous agency in how we respond. My prayer is that *Marriage in the Middle* will inspire and motivate you to do whatever it takes so that you will be able to sail resolutely and joyfully into the final chapter of life.

CHAPTER ONE

THE PARADOX OF MIDLIFE MARRIAGE

Crisis or Opportunity?

Without even trying, my husband, Christopher, and I confronted almost every major midlife challenge in an extremely compressed period of time. When we dropped off our eldest son for his first year of college, we naively assumed that we were entering midlife's sweet spot. In reality, we were saying goodbye to life as we knew it—and not in a way we would have chosen.

After settling him into his dorm, we drove east for seven hours. As we pulled into the hotel parking lot, an inebriated woman staggered out the front doors slurring, "Run! Get outta here." We thought she was talking to an imaginary friend, but in retrospect she was warning us. While packing up the next morning, a small, moving object caught my eye. I instinctively grabbed it, popped it in an empty Ziplock bag, and typed *bedbug* into my handheld. My heart sank as the photos appeared.

The hotel manager assured us that putting our belongings in commercial clothes dryers would kill the bugs. He was wrong, but it took several weeks to figure that out. We piled into the minivan completely oblivious to how much collateral damage his ignorance would cost.

Upon crossing the New York-Massachusetts border, my husband's sister called to inform us that their mom had been admitted to the hospital. We debated going back but decided that it was probably nothing serious and continued on our way to Boston.

Within an hour of arriving home, I went to the laundromat and dried all of our clothes to a crisp. All for naught. Two weeks later, we woke up with bites on our legs.

We then hired a bedbug-sniffing beagle who unceremoniously sat down in three separate places, confirming what we suspected. The pest removal specialist arrived shortly thereafter with massive portable heaters to bake each room. It looked like the Drug Enforcement Agency had come through: mattresses were pushed off the beds, chairs were turned upside down, and the contents of our closets and dressers were strewn across the room so they could be evenly cooked. The price tag exceeded two mortgage payments, and the hotel refused to share the fee.

Meanwhile, my mother-in-law's health steadily worsened. Doctors initially thought she was suffering from kidney stones. Then pancreatitis. Finally, she was diagnosed with advanced pancreatic cancer. She never made it home from the hospital.

Next up, our youngest son took a shot to the neck while playing football, resulting in a concussion and a peculiar throat injury. We spent several weeks going back and forth to specialists exploring whether or not he'd need corrective surgery. He didn't, but the injury ended his football career.

If you can believe it, things got worse.

For fifteen years Christopher had been on staff with an amazing, dynamic church. Though we both loved partnering with and serving these faith-filled men and women, we had been sensing that this chapter was coming to a close. The same week we returned from burying his mother, it became clear we needed to leave. Two months later, Christopher resigned with no next job lined up. Though I work full-time, my annual income could only cover our living expenses if we moved someplace significantly less expensive. Like a campground. In Florida.

All of this took place over three short months.

In the midst of this unraveling, I had a dream in which the two of us were hanging onto the edge of a cliff. I looked over at him and said, "I hope you're doing okay because I can't do anything to help you." It was not uncommon for us to experience four of the five stages of grief—denial, anger, bargaining, and depression—in one week. Though we prayed, talking with God did not free us from anxiety or fear. Some days, keeping the faith meant choosing not to quit.

Prior to these events, we felt competent and stable. As often happens during a crisis, the tremors exposed preexisting fault lines. Christopher began to experience the natural insecurities that come from a sudden, midcareer job loss. Doubts about his capacity and worth—things he thought he had laid to rest in his twenties—came roaring back. Those feelings propelled him into anxious activism that crowded out the boys and me. His concerns were not unfounded; there was a lot on the line. Because I deemed Christopher's experiences more consequential—and because I felt so overwhelmed—I shut down emotionally and marched resolutely through my days.

It was the most traumatic, destabilizing year we had gone through as a married couple. And yet this experience birthed deep transformation. Our crisis revealed itself as an opportunity to evaluate our life and make significant changes. My hunch is that we're not outliers. There is much wisdom to be gleaned from tumult.

REFRAMING MIDLIFE CRISIS

Even though the years between forty and sixty-five do not represent the true middle of our lives—few of us will live to one hundred or beyond—midlife is a very real thing. There's something essential going on that's worth exploring, particularly as it relates to marriage.

This is a time of multidimensional change. As these shifts alter the landscapes of our lives, it can be disturbing and raise more questions than answers. Our disorientation gets exacerbated if strategies and coping mechanisms that previously served us no longer seem to work. When what's familiar fails, we may find ourselves withdrawing, blaming, or fixating on relational dynamics that we previously overlooked. If any of this resonates with you, rest assured, you're not alone.

Psychologist Elliott Jaques introduced the term *midlife crisis* in 1965. It's no surprise that his discoveries about the inner turmoil that results from confronting one's mortality coincided with the external turmoil of the 1960s, which included racial unrest, political corruption, the Vietnam War, and multiple assassinations. More than fifty years later the concept has taken on a life of its own. Culture has come to accept this much ballyhooed term as an unavoidable reality that lurks in the shadows, waiting for an opportune moment to sabotage our lives. But is that an accurate description of midlife, or is it unhelpfully fatalistic and passive?

Journalist Barbara Bradley Hagerty sees midlife through a far more hopeful frame of renewal: "This is a time when you shift gears—a temporary pause, yes, but not a prolonged stall. In fact, you are moving forward to a new place in life. This moment can be exhilarating rather than terrifying, informed by the experiences of your past and shaped by the promise of your future."

As Christopher and I discovered, the crises that we encounter in midlife don't have to result in unhappiness, dissatisfaction, or isolation. They can help us and our marriages to grow stronger.

Psychologist and author Mary Pipher identifies the "challenges and joys" of this stage as "catalytic." She believes the seeming contradictions of this season create "a portal for expanding our souls." The divergent experiences that we're being thrust into can stimulate the kind of character development necessary to prevent us and our marriages from getting stuck or disintegrating. To get the most benefit from these soul-expanding experiences, we have to be willing to acknowledge those places where our marriages are currently fragile or even failing. And of course, an acknowledgment is not enough. We have to address those vulnerabilities with purpose and commitment.

THREE ESSENTIAL TRAITS

As we embark on this work, three qualities become imperative: malleability, resilience, and engagement. These three are not the only attributes that we need to navigate marriage in the middle of life, but they helped Christopher and me to make it through our year from hell.

Malleability fosters transformation. In the physical world a metal's malleability is directly related to how much pressure it can withstand without snapping. Midlife is an extended season of pressure. If we're malleable, the sustained stress will result in something new and good. If we resist change, we're in danger of relational and spiritual rigidity.

We become increasingly malleable as we flex and adapt in the face of health scares, financial dilemmas, professional disappointments, family conflicts, etc. Malleability should help us to learn how far we can stretch and what happens when we overextend.

Whereas malleability is the willingness to be stretched and changed, resilience determines how quickly we'll bounce back after something difficult or trying has happened. Facebook executive Sheryl Sandberg defines *resilience* as "the strength and speed of our response to adversity." The Japanese have a proverb that explains resilience: *Nana korobi Ya oki*, which means "fall down seven times but get up eight." In other words, persevere. Don't quit.

Resilience is one measure of maturity. Children learn to be resilient when they have nurturing, caring parents (or caregivers) who teach them how to rebound after they've made mistakes or suffered losses. Even if we lacked those necessary ingredients when we were growing up, we can still become resilient by cultivating supportive relationships, choosing hope, and refusing to see ourselves as powerless victims.

Whether it's the death of our parents, infertility, or loss of employment, we will all have the wind knocked out of us. But there's no stopping the clock or taking time-outs in midlife. Our world might be shaken and our ego deeply bruised. We might even forget all the things we've done well. But after we've had a good cry (or a good sulk) and caught our breath, we have to get up and get back in the game because our spouses and our families need us.

Malleability and resilience presuppose that we're engaged. Engagement means paying attention and remaining actively involved. The antithesis of engagement is passivity, withdrawal, or apathy—none of which work well in a high-stakes season like midlife.

The challenges of this time frame require us to be present in every sphere. If we're parents, our children don't need less of us as they get older; they need us in different capacities. After needing us peripherally or perhaps not at all for most of their lives, our mothers and fathers will increasingly look to us for emotional, practical, and spiritual support. Because of the chaotic nature of midlife, our spouses will continue to need comfort and reassurance.

Becoming more malleable, resilient, and engaged won't simply help us to be better people: these attributes may actually prevent marital failure.

A CATALYST FOR CHANGE

In the course of that one disastrous year, Christopher and I had to navigate what felt like a decade's worth of loss and disappointment. Though the events shook us to the core, they also presented us with opportunities to trust God more deeply. Each time the bottom fell out, we had a sense of God's presence. Sometimes he held our hands during the free fall and sometimes he met us at the bottom, but he was always there and always helped us to heal and reconnect. Thanks to his abiding presence, we found our way through the losses and emerged more in love and more certain that choosing to marry each other was one of the best decisions we'd ever made.

The two of us have had to work hard for the marriage we now enjoy. Before we got married, Christopher and I had so much conflict that friends predicted a tumultuous first year. For the record, that first year exceeded our expectations. It was year ten that nearly sunk us. We're both chronically opinionated and strong willed, which has its benefits and drawbacks. We've raised our voices, shamed each other, and withheld affection in the worst possible moments. In other words, we're normal people who often fail.

Yet here we are in our late fifties, still appreciating each other's company, still discovering new things, still having great sex, and still excited about following Jesus together. Christopher and I have spent enough time counseling and pastoring other couples to know that not all marriages land where we have. Couples dig in their heels. Instead of acknowledging their contribution to the problems, they blame each other and either endlessly cycle around the same conflicts or lose their will to fight.

There's no simple explanation for why we've made it and why other couples haven't because we're all under unique stress during this time period. That does not mean we will inevitably spin out or land in despair. One of the gifts of midlife is learning to recognize our own limitations and then extending grace to ourselves—and others. Especially our spouse. In fact, by choosing to accept and fully embrace our limited spouse, we can actually experience greater intimacy (both emotional and physical), deeper trust, and more fulfilling friendship.

It's true that the disruptive nature of midlife can leave us longing for peace and stability. That said, perhaps the opposite of crisis is neither peace nor stability. Maybe it's discovery. And maybe the key for us is to use the crises as impetus to grow. My hope is that all of us will not only make it through this season with our marriages intact, but experience profound transformation and joy in the midst of it. This book is an invitation to join me on that journey.

GOING DEEPER

1. What's surprised you about midlife? What's been harder than you anticipated? What's been easier or welcome?

2. How have the challenges of midlife invited you to change?

3. What is it like to realize that you're at the halfway point of your life or even beyond? Are you energized? Discouraged? Hopeful? What are you looking forward to in the second half of your life? What are you fearing or even dreading?

4. If malleability, resilience, and engagement are key to thriving in midlife, how are you doing in each of these areas? Where would you like to grow? What might that growth look like?

CHAPTER TWO

TELOS

What Was, What Is, and What's to Come

While Scot and Camille were working overseas, they had a car accident that claimed the life of their seven-year-old daughter. Three decades later their son lost his battle with cancer in his mid-thirties. In between those two tragic losses, Camille had an affair and a ministry partner embezzled their retirement funds.

Any one of those heartaches could capsize a marriage, but Scot and Camille never gave up on their relationship or on the church. Now both in their seventies, they are two of the most remarkable human beings I've ever met. They're winsome, wise, and completely engaged in every aspect of life. Until recently, they both did pastoral care at their church.

Camille observes, "We've now been married for fifty years, and we can honestly say that we enjoy and understand one another more than ever before. We feel close to Jesus and experience his joy, direction, and peace through the Holy Spirit on a daily basis."

Though none of us would ever choose to walk in their footsteps, my guess is that we all hope to experience similar contentedness and connectedness in the last chapter of our lives. Given that every marriage is unique, we can't fabricate a formula based on Scot and Camille's success and assume it will work for us. But we can glean

practices and principles. Scot and Camille got through their challenges and emerged in a better, healthier place because they rooted
themselves in God's historic provision, went deeper in their faith,
and then allowed the Holy Spirit to lead them toward something new.

THE PAST

Our histories play an important role in our marriages, particularly
when storms are raging. The twenty-one years that Christopher and
I had together served as ballast to keep us from capsizing during that
season of loss. We remembered how God helped us to forgive each
other during our broken engagement. We remembered how he led
us to take a first-time homebuyers' class that enabled us to purchase
a house with a mere 5 percent down payment and no closing costs.
We recalled the many adventures and trials that shaped our marriage. The more we remembered, the more fortified we felt.

To some degree, our pasts conjugate our present and future tenses.
"We engage our memories in tandem with God," writes pastor and
spiritual director Casey Tygrett, "because they are the starting points
for who we are now and who we have yet to become." We're not necessarily bound by the past, but it definitely shapes our todays and
our tomorrows. In fact, looking back can help us to move forward.

Judaism has much to teach us about the role of our histories and
the power of remembering. Perhaps because of the many times the
Jewish people have been persecuted, they understand the importance
of recalling God's faithfulness. Certain holidays, such as Purim and
Passover, facilitate community-wide opportunities to remember. Additionally, several millennia ago the Hebrews crafted tangible altars
to keep their memories alive. These visual reminders made it impossible for them to forget God's faithful provision. The Old Testament
book of Joshua recounts how one of these altars came to be.

For forty years God miraculously sustained Moses and the twelve
tribes of Israel as they escaped from slavery and wandered toward

the Promised Land. After Moses died, Joshua became the new leader. On the last leg of their epic journey, the Israelites came to a full stop at the swollen Jordan River. There was no bridge or ferry, and we can assume it was not swimmable. But God once again proved that nothing can thwart his purposes.

The moment the priest carrying the Ark of the Covenant stepped into the river, the water stopped flowing, allowing them to pass on dry ground. God then directed Joshua to have one representative from each tribe take a stone from the middle of the Jordan, put it on their shoulder, and "build a memorial" out of them so that in the future when their children asked about the memorial, they could say, "'They remind us that the Jordan River stopped flowing when the Ark of the LORD's Covenant went across.' These stones will stand as a memorial among the people of Israel forever" (Joshua 4:1-7).

Unlike the Jewish faith, contemporary Christianity by and large fails to provide traditions that help us to remember God's supernatural provision and protection. Therefore, we have to be more intentional. The Psalms provide one example of what this might look like.

In Psalm 77 the author admits that he's in a difficult space and seems to feel forgotten by God:

> When I was in deep trouble,
>   I searched for the Lord.
> All night long I prayed, with hands lifted toward heaven,
>   but my soul was not comforted.
> I think of God, and I moan,
>   overwhelmed with longing for his help. (vv. 2-3)

Then there's a pivot:

> But then I *recall* all you have done, O LORD;
>   I *remember* your wonderful deeds of long ago.
> They are constantly in my thoughts.
>   I *cannot stop thinking* about your mighty works.

O God, your ways are holy.
　Is there any god as mighty as you?
You are the God of great wonders!
　You demonstrate your awesome power among the nations.
By your strong arm, you redeemed your people,
　the descendants of Jacob and Joseph.
　　(vv. 11-15, emphasis added)

The psalmist chooses to remember God's character, which puts the brakes on his descent into despair. He then encounters hope. Just as the psalmist's words inspire and encourage us today, when we tell others how God has come through in our lives, we not only refresh our own memories but bring encouragement to those who may be standing on the banks of the Jordan waiting for God to part the waters.

During the turbulent year that Christopher and I went through, God's faithfulness became our own personal "stone of remembrance," which provided the sustenance we needed to keep going. As we build and revisit memorials to God's faithfulness, we begin to see a distinct through line that serves three purposes: it fills us with faith and hope, it brings us clarity about the future, and it shifts the focus from our weakness to his magnificent strength.

THE PRESENT

Sanctification: The process of becoming. Looking back should not result in regret or romanticizing what was. It should help us to root ourselves in God so we can grow toward Christ and do the heavy lifting that this season requires of us. The term *sanctification* is a helpful descriptor for that rooting and growing.

Sanctification involves "being fundamentally changed in the depths of our being so that the will of God can be done *in our lives* on earth as it is in heaven." Fundamental change is a lifelong process. Becoming more like Christ and less selfish, less impatient, less lazy, less whatever requires years of work and prayer. As my friend Rebecca reminds me, "There are no shortcuts for sanctification."

One aspect of sanctification is reordering our desires. This happens not by cutting ourselves off from desire but by developing an increasingly intimate relationship with God, which then allows us to align our hearts and minds with his will. As we do this, we find that we want God's kingdom more than the offerings of the world. Instead of filling ourselves with sugar or carbs when we're feeling sad, we turn to God and our spouse to meet our need for comfort. Instead of overinvesting in work, we confess our anxieties about the future, learn what it looks like to trust God more fully, and redirect more of our creative energies toward the people we love.

The long-term nature of sanctification can be wearisome and discouraging, in part because we sometimes wonder if change will ever come. In my experience, we can spend years wanting and trying to change particular behaviors or thought patterns with little measurable success. And then one day the work pays off. It's like the atmosphere changes. There's an openness, a grace, and because we're empowered by the Holy Spirit, something suddenly shifts.

As I was writing this section, outside my office window I noticed an oak sapling pinned to the ground by an early, wet snowfall. A slight breeze blew across the yard, and the sapling quivered. The snow fell off in a big plop, and the little oak snapped upright. That's a *suddenly*. When these suddenlies happen, it's unmistakable and welcome, particularly to our spouse. Whether we've been faithfully following Jesus for decades or just started last week, we can all experience radical change because the Holy Spirit is available to everyone.

The Holy Spirit: Our faithful companion. The Holy Spirit functions as our direct link to Jesus and God the Father. The Spirit is distinct from both but coequal. According to Scripture, the Holy Spirit is our comforter, guide, teacher, intercessor, and the guarantee of our salvation. At the Last Supper, Jesus explained how his imminent departure would ultimately benefit not only his disciples but all of his followers for generations to come: "I will ask the Father, and he will give you another Advocate, who will never leave you. He is the Holy Spirit, who leads into all truth" (John 14:16-17).

Upon deciding to follow Christ, we receive the Holy Spirit. Some faith traditions teach that there is a one-time filling that lasts for our entire lives. Other traditions teach that we can get topped off, for lack of a better explanation, by simply asking for more. Whatever your personal belief, the idea of being filled by or with the Holy Spirit seems to imply that we have to make space for this person of the Trinity (see Acts 2 and Ephesians 5:18 for more on this). By reordering our desires and moving toward Christ, we displace sin and free up more room for the Spirit.

When Camille and Scot immersed themselves in church cultures that valued the Holy Spirit, Camille felt compelled to confess her long-held secret and end the affair. This breakthrough changed the trajectory of their life. As Camille discovered, pursuing sanctification and embracing the Holy Spirit make us increasingly—and often uncomfortably—aware of any idolatry (which is a form of disordered attachment).

Identifying and breaking free from our idols. We might be tempted to dismiss idol worship as an ancient practice that has little or no relevance in the twenty-first century. That would be a mistake. We're all vulnerable to idolatry. Our hearts are made to worship and if we do not bow down to our Creator, we bow down to the created. God knows this. That's why the very first commandment instructs us to forsake all other gods (Deuteronomy 5:7).

Idols not only vie for the limited real estate in our hearts, they intend to evict God. Idols can be people (particularly those who carry power and influence such as celebrities and politicians), objects (such as electronic devices or cars), and things we invest our time and energy in (such as careers or sporting events). Most of the people, activities, or objects are not intrinsically evil nor do they have power over us in and of themselves (assuming we're not talking about political dictators or Sauron's ring). Demonic forces prop them up, and they gain control when we habitually trust and value them above God. When we're sober and objective, we know it's foolish to depend on idols rather than on God. So why do we fall for it?

Human nature prefers easy. And let's be honest; it's often much easier to eat ice cream, drink a few glasses of wine, or practice retail therapy than acknowledge our emotional pain and talk about it with someone. Even if that someone is our spouse. Our proclivity toward idolatrous behavior makes more sense when we realize that the idol's promise often represents (or symbolizes) a legitimate need. For example, the pursuit of money might indicate a felt need for security and safety. A preoccupation with certain types of food or women's breasts might suggest a need for comfort.

No one aspires to become an idolater, and typically, the objects of our affection don't become idols overnight. Our relationship with sports, money, food, sex, social media, or whatever usually starts out quite innocently and shifts over time. This can make it difficult for us to notice when we cross over into idolatrous behaviors. One of the ways we can identify the presence of an idol in our lives is by paying attention to what we think about, where we spend our money, and how we react when the object of our adoration becomes unavailable. One could say that the 2020 pandemic gave us plenty of opportunities to topple our idols because so many of the things we normally depend on for comfort and security were stripped away.

What we inevitably discover after a season of kneeling before our small-g-gods is that we're dissatisfied and angry. This makes sense because we've been deceived. Idols always overpromise and underdeliver. Our God-given spiritual and relational needs for security, comfort, companionship, and love can only be satisfied by our Creator and in the context of healthy relationships. If we don't truly believe this fundamental truth, we will probably continue chasing idols. That plays out in a myriad of ways, including through broken expressions of sexuality and unreflective consumerism.

Sexual idolatry has ancient roots. That's part of why it's so powerful. One of the idols mentioned in Scripture and other ancient Near Eastern literature is Baal, a fertility god. You might recall how Baal's prophets lost the remarkable showdown with Elijah as recounted in 1 Kings 18. Worship of this god included temple prostitution and human sacrifice. The enemy took something that God created and blessed—sex—and fused it with the abuse of power, destruction, and murder.

Engaging in sexual behavior with anyone other than our spouse not only violates trust but also causes excruciating pain. However, because we live in a hypersexualized culture and because there are so many stressors and insecurities in midlife, we are particularly vulnerable to sexual idolatry's promise of escape and pleasure. When we engage in idolatrous behaviors, we're not simply choosing to ignore God's boundaries—we're saying we know better and trusting our judgment over God's. This never ends well. Particularly as it pertains to our sexuality.

The longer we chase after the idol, the more deceived we become. Camille couldn't see this until after she ended the affair, but her desires had become disordered. She didn't want sex; she wanted affirmation, attention, and affection from her husband. The affair temporarily distracted her from her pain and disappointment, but it failed to deliver what she really needed. This is always true of idols.

Like sexual idolatry, consumerism constantly pulls at us. As the pop icon Madonna crooned back in the '80s, we live in a material world. The idea that buying and owning lead to popularity, power, and happiness has been etched into the American psyche. Shopping is part of our civic responsibility. That's how we keep our capitalistic economy afloat. Perhaps the most blatant example of consumerism is Black Friday, when bargain hunters camp out in the parking lots of big box stores and forget all the rules of civility when the doors open Friday morning. It's ironic that this happens less than twenty-four hours after the one day of the year set aside for us to be thankful.

Meeting our needs while avoiding the "tiny parasite" called greed is complicated. We can't live without material goods, which drives us into stores. While there, we happen to notice those cute shoes, the latest iPhone, and the still-warm donuts. Noticing leads to wanting, which leads to justifying, which leads to impulse buying and, sometimes, hoarding. (I'm preaching to myself here. I currently own twenty-one pairs of shoes and boots.) If we hope to purge the parasite of greed from our system and curtail unnecessary buying, we will have to regularly repent and choose gratitude. Even when our lives do not measure up to cultural ideals. After all, contentment is not a commodity. It's a choice.

From birth to death, we are being wooed by God and seduced by the enemy. This ongoing battle has epic consequences for our marriage. If we say yes to God, he will draw our focus outward and empower us to love and serve our spouse. By comparison, pursuing idols makes us inherently self-centered and thwarts our ability to love and serve others. Choosing between the two warring factions should be easy. But as many of us will attest, that's not necessarily true. The apostle Paul explains why: "We are not fighting against flesh-and-blood enemies, but against evil rulers and authorities of the unseen world, against mighty powers in this dark world, and against evil spirits in the heavenly places" (Ephesians 6:12). We're naive if we discount this. Based on how Satan played Adam and Eve, he's intent on turning us away from God and each other. This is because healthy marriages uniquely reveal the kingdom of God on earth—something that Satan hates.

If we fail to recognize and repent of our idolatrous habits, we will be blown off course by the winds of deception, *and we don't have time for that*. There's an urgency about midlife. Mistakes are much more consequential now. The fallout from our choices affects more people. There's less time to regroup and recoup our losses. But we need better motivation than warnings and the threat of dire consequences if we hope to renounce idolatry. We need hope and vision for our future.

THE FUTURE: CULTIVATING OUR IMAGINATION

The late Yogi Berra, famed manager of the New York Yankees and master of nonsensical one-liners, is reported to have said, "If you don't know where you're going, you'll end up someplace else." This is both ridiculous and profound, particularly as it pertains to life at the halfway point. We can avoid losing our way in midlife by clarifying our hoped-for destination. The concept of telos may help us to parse out what this looks like.

Telos comes from the ancient Greek language. It's an unfamiliar word for most of us and not one that we'll immediately fold into our vocabulary. It's worth wrestling with because there's no English equivalent and the concept of telos serves the conversation about our future.

Telos means "fulfillment," "end," or the "end goal" of an intentional process. But it's not simply a fixed point at the end of a line. As it relates to midlife marriage, telos is our ultimate destination, the specific path that we take, *and* how we love and serve those who journey with us. If we think about the purpose of a family vacation, it's not checking in at an ocean-front Airbnb. It's a process that includes deciding *together* where the family wants to go, picking out restaurants and day trips, the excitement of packing suitcases, the three-hour walk along a dramatic beach, the deepening of relationships, and the memories that we hold on to for years to come. A helpful way to think about telos is that it's "a guiding purpose."

This purpose-driven understanding of telos means *how* we get where we're going is every bit as significant as the end goal. And the journey is rarely linear, which means we have to notice when we're heading into a storm and recalibrate as needed. Like airplane pilots.

When pilots fly from the East Coast to the West Coast, they don't simply put the desired destination into their flight computer, climb to cruising altitude, and read a book. They're constantly monitoring flight conditions, checking in with regional air traffic control centers, and reprogramming their in-flight computers as necessary. If the plane is heading into bad weather, the captain may manually override the autopilot. These ongoing check-ins and adjustments allow pilots to fine-tune their flight and avoid unnecessary turbulence.

I think we would agree that all marriages would benefit from less turbulence. In-flight marital check-ins might include asking each other questions such as *what's working, what's not working,* or *where are we stuck*? It should also include regularly and proactively confessing our sins and adapting our behaviors based on the changing needs of our family. Occasionally, some check-ins might determine that the turbulence can't be avoided, and therefore, everyone simply needs to fasten their seat belts and ride it out. That was our twenty-first year.

We can't reach any destination by simply making a one-time decision. To avoid ending up where we have no intention or desire to go, we must routinely determine if we're on course and recalibrate when needed. We have to fly the plane. And as any good pilot will tell you, navigation requires creativity and imagination.

It's no exaggeration to say that we need our imaginations in every phase and every aspect of life. A robust imagination is essential to figure out how to use the kohlrabi in our farm share, remodel the bathroom, pay for college, and sustain a healthy marriage.

Engaging our imaginations and living creatively should not be seen as child's play or as a privilege for select vocations such as artist or author. To think along these lines is to deny our heritage. Poet Luci Shaw asserts, "We who believe we bear God's image must realize that the image includes the capacity to imagine and create, because God is himself an imaginative Creator."

In fact, God is the ultimate Creator. The Trinity came up with the idea for giant sequoias, watermelons, rainbows, hummingbirds, dolphins, and the particulars of procreation. The Trinity also decided that every snowflake and every human should be unique. You may not write novels or paint portraits, but you have the capacity to bring order, solve problems, and make beautiful things, which is what being creative is all about.

A vibrant, rooted-in-God imagination also serves our relationships, particularly marriage and parenting. There are many times in the course of our lives when we feel stuck. In these situations, imagining something new is, in and of itself, "an act of hope." When we imagine what our marriage might look like in five or ten years, we are choosing to believe that there is a future and we have some agency in it. This confronts any of the powerlessness or hopelessness that linger because the specifics we had previously imagined did not come to pass or because we're being told—subtly and sometimes not so subtly—that the world does not want what we have to offer.

Walter Brueggemann, one of the most influential Old Testament scholars of the twenty-first century, writes, "The task of the prophetic imagination . . . is to cut through the despair and to penetrate the dissatisfied coping that seems to have no end or resolution." Our imaginations should be able to transcend the present moment, even when hope is waning or circumstances portend doom because it's God's power and inexhaustible hope that fuel our imagination.

Faith and imagination are synergistic. None of us have ever seen God face-to-face. To step over the line from unbelief to belief, we must extrapolate who God is based on the knowledge we've gleaned from Scripture, others' testimonies, and our personal experiences of encountering Jesus. Since none of these prove the existence of God, the Holy Spirit inspires our imagination—or faith—tipping the balance away from doubt toward belief.

In the same way that a faith-filled imagination can help us to move from skepticism to faith in our relationship with God, it can help us move from unhappiness or dissatisfaction to contentment and delight in our marriages. Sometimes, this can be as simple as a quick prayer: "God, help me to see our potential. Help me believe that change is possible." And then waiting in holy anticipation. Sometimes it takes years of hard work, counseling, extended prayer, and staying present in the seemingly impossible moments.

To ignite our imaginations and keep them burning, we need to understand the role of criticism because nothing douses our imagination more quickly than incessant or insensitive critique.

In the process of writing this book I've had to make thousands of critical decisions. This word, this idea, not that one. I've had to delete some of my favorite paragraphs. There's no morality and few emotions attached to these choices. I don't have to worry about hurting anyone's feelings as I edit. Criticism is a lot trickier in the relational realm.

Though criticism is an essential component of the creative process, it's also inherently dangerous. Most of us are skilled in identifying—sometimes to the millimeter—what's wrong with our spouse, our in-laws, our pastor. And typically we don't stop at identifying the problem: we home in on it, magnify it, and often make biased and unfair conclusions because of it. Sadly, we seem to have cataracts regarding our own flaws. If we fail to understand the extenuating circumstance or how we may have contributed to the issue, our criticism will most likely be inaccurate, unhelpful, and possibly even damaging.

For instance, Scot's judgment of Camille contributed to her vulnerability toward other men. He felt she was not as spiritual as he was. Rather than imagining together how she might become more engaged, he judged and criticized her. For criticism to be productive, it needs to move beyond focusing on the problem to finding solutions.

Experiencing a disappointing vacation, having multiple unproductive fights, or feeling a vague sense of malaise can all be starting points for imagining something new and recalibrating our telos. Thankfully, this is the direction that Scot and Camille took after they broke free from idolatry. Their story is both heartbreaking and inspiring.

⌒

How did your daughter's death affect your marriage?

CAMILLE   Our life would never be the same. I cried myself to sleep for about three years. Scot and I grieved so differently. I wanted to talk about our daughter all the time, but he was too sad to even mention her name. When the other kids went off to school, I would eat chocolate and stare out the window. More than forty years have gone by since that accident, and to this day when we think about our daughter, we are often brought to tears.

SCOT   I kept busy teaching school, jogging, and trying to hold the family together. Eight years later, I was in counseling and finally mentioned her death. I sobbed uncontrollably for two hours.

Zooming ahead to midlife, where did you find yourselves as a couple?

CAMILLE   I felt Scot was more interested in our church and our pastor than he was in me. I remember one day when a friend stopped by looking for Scot. I knew he was with our leader rather than at home, and I got so angry because he was always working for him. This had been going on for years. I'd had it. It was around this time that a man at work showed interest in me. I liked the attention. This was the beginning of the affair. I told

Scot that I was interested in someone else, but I didn't tell him everything.

SCOT This was a total shock. I spent the night walking the streets. We needed help, but at first Camille was unwilling. Eventually, she agreed, and we went to a counselor. He got me to see that Camille did not feel cherished and that I was a big part of the problem. I was constantly criticizing her and putting pressure on her to be more spiritual. We spent the next couple of years in counseling, and this helped.

But we were very dry spiritually and sought out churches where God was moving. We had encounters with the Holy Spirit, and out of this we were given new hope, power, and insight into how we could heal and grow.

CAMILLE We spent a lot of time worshiping and praying together. We felt closer to God and more connected to each other than ever before. Though we were doing better, there were still some secrets that hadn't been shared.

The Holy Spirit brought conviction, and we finally were able to be completely honest with each other. I was able to tell Scot that I had a sexual affair, and he was able to tell me that he had been overly invested in a platonic but emotionally unhealthy relationship with another woman. We were able to forgive one another and work through that. This did not happen overnight.

(Not long after they had worked through their affairs, their adult son was diagnosed with stage-four colon cancer.) Once again, you found yourselves facing every parent's worst nightmare. What role did your faith play?

SCOT   We found strength by drawing closer to God and sensing his presence day by day, moment by moment. By asking God for more of his presence and clinging to him, we were able to keep our heads above water and not drown in a sea of grief.

CAMILLE   Losing a child is no easier the second time. I remember a conversation I had with our son a few weeks before he died. He said, "Mom, I'm really sorry you have to go through this a second time." I couldn't respond then, but the next day I told him, "Of course I want you to live, but if you do die, we will be okay because God will be faithful to us, just like he was when your sister died. And he will be faithful to your family. Your kids will be okay!" This was helpful even though the grief still makes me cry as I write this, ten years later.

Even as your son was succumbing to cancer, you never gave up—on your marriage, on God, or on the church. How was that possible?

SCOT   The traumas we've been through created a hunger in us for more of God. He took us out of our comfort zone. When we both decided that we wanted more of Jesus, the Holy Spirit ambushed us with his tangible presence in a way that was practical, simple, and life-changing. Our marriage took on a new direction after this. There was more joy and peace. We didn't take life so seriously. We started praying more, especially for others, and we devoured the Scripture.

CAMILLE   The reality of God's presence and his love for us was undeniable. We couldn't walk away from that. And because God is in the business of redeeming everything, for the past twenty years we've been able to help

other couples imagine how they can experience
freedom from their past and create healthier marriages!

∽⚬

By embracing the Holy Spirit and choosing to remember the many
ways God had proven himself faithful, Scot and Camille drew closer
to each other and to God. Rather than succumbing to despair or
giving up, they imagined and then created a new path. God's love
and resurrection power make this possible for all of us—regardless
of where we are today or what's coming over the horizon.

GOING DEEPER

1. If there are any places in your marriage where you feel stuck or
   have lost hope, when and how did that happen? What would it
   take for you to identify and own your contribution to the issue
   and then talk about this as a couple?

2. The late theologian Eugene Peterson believed that "if we keep the
   first commandment well and the last commandment well, all the
   commandments between are protected: love God, love your
   neighbor." How are you doing keeping the first and last commandments? What about all the commandments in between? Where
   would you like to grow?

3. Do you have any desires that need to be reordered? What core
   needs or longings are the disordered desires masking? How might
   reordering these desires draw you closer to God and your spouse?

4. What's your understanding of the Holy Spirit's role in your life
   and more specifically in your marriage? How could you become
   more connected to the Holy Spirit?

5. What has the process of sanctification looked like for you? Where
   has your marriage revealed places where you need to grow? How
   are you pursuing that growth?

CHAPTER THREE

CH, CH, CH, CHANGES

*Reading Glasses, Receding Hairlines,
and Reorganized Hormones*

The same week Carol learned she was pregnant with their second
child, her husband, Bill, was diagnosed with cancer. Tests confirmed it was a lemon-sized tumor on the base of his tongue—an
incredibly difficult place to operate. The news hit hard. According
to Carol,

> It all happened really fast. I had moments when I felt like,
> "Okay, this is no biggie. The prognosis is great. We can do this,"
> and other moments that were pretty dire. It was the first time
> I'd ever really needed to confront my own mortality and that
> of my spouse. Being pregnant made it hurt more: I had many
> unhealthy daydreams about the fate of our family.
>
> After the diagnosis we shot into action. We were constantly
> going to doctor's appointments. I remember one morning we
> went from an oncologist's appointment to our first fetal ultra-
> sound. It was a weird day.

Not many couples will find themselves going back and forth between cancer treatments and prenatal checkups in midlife. However,
this is a time marked by an uptick in doctors' visits and preventative

screenings: a reality that forces us to reckon with our visibly changing bodies. As we hit menopause and andropause (the seldom talked about changes that happen for men), we may get ambushed by depression, panic attacks, or insomnia. We will have to adjust our calorie intake to accommodate a slower metabolism. Some of us will be on a first-name basis with physical therapists after having our joints replaced. Others will bear scars from far more consequential surgeries. Daunting? That's putting it mildly.

Our health affects every aspect of marriage—from our ability to perform household chores, to our earning potential, to sex. As such, we cannot afford to dismiss or downplay the unique physical and mental health needs of midlife. By making peace with our increasing limitations and learning how to care for ourselves and each other, we should be able to experience aging as a blessing rather than a curse.

OUR CHANGING BODIES

Since 1900, remarkable advances in health care and disease prevention, coupled with an increased understanding of how diet and lifestyle affect us, have added approximately thirty years to our life span. I'm so grateful. I would hate to think about death being imminent as I turn sixty. That said, these additional decades are not without their challenges and concerns, including menopause and andropause, sleep issues, chronic pain, and ongoing physical and mental health issues.

Menopause and andropause. Those of you in your early forties may not have to think about menopause or andropause for five to ten years. Enjoy that time because compared to all the other transitions that are part of midlife, nothing else has such comprehensive effects as our changing hormones. Though we tend to reduce hormones to those pesky drivers of irresponsible teenage behavior, they have been working nonstop since the moment we were conceived. Without them we would die. Consummate communicators, hormones carry "messages to and from all organs of the body and serve to connect one organ's function with another organ's function to keep the body balanced and functioning optimally." Among other roles, hormones control the body's metabolism; stimulate arousal and hunger; and regulate brain, nerve, and muscle function.

Women generally reach menopause in their early- to mid-fifties, which means we have experienced our menses for thirty to forty years. Each month our hormones shift, causing any or all of the following symptoms: cramping, bloating, headaches, weight gain, sleep disturbances, migraines, and mood swings. By now, our monthly friend has visited more than three hundred times, and frankly most of us are ready to end the relationship and move on. That said, women who wanted to be biological mothers but who have never given birth may feel deep grief about the finality that menopause represents.

Segueing into midlife has its own trials. As the ovaries reduce their estrogen output and slip gracefully into retirement, disrupted sleep, dryness (everywhere!), decreased libido, hot flashes, night sweats, brain fog, weight gain, and personality changes may begin. Symptoms vary and depend on any number of factors, including overall health, stress levels, diet, smoking and drinking habits, and exercise—or lack thereof.

Because I'm an avid reader and have older friends, I anticipated every symptom of menopause. Except for the anger. Up to this point, I had been anger-avoidant—especially with men. Menopause changed that.

The misogynistic microaggressions that I had tolerated for the past fifty years became intolerable. When men referred to me as a girl, I corrected them. If they told crude jokes in my presence, I asked them to stop. Being nice was no longer a priority. Christopher has always appreciated how anger gives him a laser-like focus. I now understand this phenomenon. Author and women's health advocate Christine Northrup concurs:

It is very common for women to become more irritable, even downright angry, about things that were more easily over-looked before. . . . It is well known that hormones modulate both aggression and anger. Our midlife bodies and brains fully support our ability to experience and express anger with a clarity not possible prior to midlife.

This newfound ability to access anger can either help or hurt our marriages. If we've been in the habit of ignoring or minimizing issues, anger can alert us that something is wrong and call us to action. Provided that we discern what it's trying to teach us and then address the problem, it can improve marital health. If we refuse to acknowledge our contribution to the dynamic or use anger as an excuse to misbehave, it can be unproductive or even damaging. To process anger well, we need to balance honesty with self-control. This can be complicated when both spouses are navigating the 'pause simultaneously.

Curiously, while women's change of life centers around the end of fertility, men's bodies can produce sperm until the end of their lives. Despite this fundamental difference, the symptoms of andropause are every bit as consequential as those of their female counterpart. The gradual drop in testosterone that starts in the late twenties be-comes more noticeable in their forties and fifties. It may result in lower energy and lower sex drive, insomnia, increased body fat, de-creased muscle strength, hair loss, prostate issues, depression, and erectile dysfunction (ED).

If men have linked their self-worth to—or defined themselves by—their energy, power, and strength, they may feel ineffectual and find themselves in the midst of an identity crisis. This has definitely been true for Christopher. He explains,

When our sons out-run and out-jump us or our junior col-leagues garner the attention and respect we once enjoyed, we can feel that we've lost ground that can never be regained. For those of us who were powerfully athletic, we have to admit we can't keep up with the former version of ourselves. For those of us who have always struggled to stay ahead of our flabby bodies, we conclude that we'll never be the man we always hoped we would become. These are sobering realizations.

Where many women think nothing of casually discussing intimate health issues like hormone treatment options, men are less likely to talk about their changing bodies. This lack of information and support makes them more vulnerable to ignoring troubling symptoms and may lead them to believe that a quick fix (e.g., Viagra) will solve their problems.

Treating hormonally related–midlife health issues is controversial. There's a chance that medication might result in other unwanted conditions or may falsely assure men that they do not need to consider the role that emotional or relational issues might be playing. For instance, ED can be caused by prostate issues or a heart condition, but it can also be attributable to depression, anxiety, or reliance on pornography. The estimated 10 percent of American men who experience ED should go to their primary care doctor, but they should also not dismiss the possibility of a mind-body connection. Regardless of the symptoms, it's helpful for couples to discuss the pros and cons of hormonal treatment together so they can find the best possible solution.

Sleep deprivation. One of the most common complaints from both men and women during midlife is disrupted sleep. Experts believe that most adults need seven to nine hours of uninterrupted sleep every night. Despite this reality, only 59 percent of Americans actually succeed in getting that much shuteye. According to a 2017 study done by the Center for Disease Control, nearly half of all women going through menopause wake up feeling unrested.

The causality of poor sleep varies. As we age, our brain waves don't have the same peaks and valleys during our sleep cycles. This translates to lighter sleep that's more easily interrupted by any number of issues, including a snoring spouse, indigestion (which occurs more frequently the older we get), the urge to urinate (caused by prostate issues for men or weakening pelvic floor muscles for women), restless legs syndrome, a glass of wine with dinner, or a sore back. Insufficient deep sleep affects way more than our morning mood. According to numerous studies, it can result in cognitive impairment, heart issues, high blood pressure, obesity, depression, and shorter life spans.

This concerns me because I've not slept through the night for more than twenty-six years. Prior to my first pregnancy, I could fall asleep instantly and stay asleep for seven to eight hours. After six years of getting up in the night with babies, my body forgot how to sleep. Then I had a long illness that triggered fibromyalgia. The chronic pain associated with fibro tends to disrupt sleep. To complicate matters, Christopher snores. His snore is not a cute, cartoon-like wuffle; it calls to mind a wild boar with a sinus infection.

Because of this, we now intermittently sleep in separate bedrooms. Sleeping together is good. It helps us to stay connected and is comforting. But not always. We were only sleeping about five hours a night and were growing increasingly irritable with each other. We always connect before retiring and have sex on a regular basis, but some nights we pull up the covers and turn out the lights in separate rooms. I'm not necessarily recommending this as a long-term solution, but it has relieved pressure in our marriage. If you choose this route for the sake of improving your sleep, please make sure that it does not become a convenient way to avoid relational issues.

Chronic pain and long-term health issues. It does not give me any comfort to know that, like me, one in ten Americans battles chronic pain. Unlike acute, short-term pain (e.g., spraining an ankle), chronic pain lasts for at least twelve weeks and generally resists normal treatment. Chronic pain can result from a car accident, degeneration of the spine, arthritis, and any number of autoimmune diseases such as Crohn's, fibromyalgia, or Lyme disease.

My pain varies between a level two and a seven. One being no pain and ten being unmedicated labor and delivery—or breaking a femur. Regardless of my pain level, I've learned that complaining and feeling sorry for myself have negative effects on everyone. As such, I tend to say little if anything. I also want to live as normally as possible. Though certain activities are now off-limits (including swimming laps and playing basketball), if you observed me on a day-to-day basis, you might never guess that pain is a constant companion.

Managing chronic pain can sometimes feel like a part-time job. For starters, although physical pain might be localized, it affects everything. When I'm in a high pain cycle, I have to deal with the actual pain (e.g., by stretching, not sitting for too long, etc.) as well as the psychological and spiritual components. To cope, I often detach. If I let myself be fully present, I can become deeply discouraged. It's hard for Christopher when I evacuate, but sometimes it's the only way I can make it through the day. Over the years I've learned to communicate what's going on so that he doesn't take it personally.

Like chronic pain, cancer and other long-term illnesses or health issues tend to radically alter a couple's relational landscape. As Carol and Bill discovered, cancer forces us to confront our mortality and turns our worlds upside down, in part because it feels so incredibly random. Yes, the likelihood of contracting cancer is greater when we smoke, drink heavily, never use sunscreen, have lots of sexual partners, or don't exercise. And yet those with a high number of risk factors may never get cancer while those who eat well, exercise, don't smoke, slather on the sunscreen, and are monogamous do. That reality can scramble our understanding of a benevolent, miracle-working God, leaving us with a faith crisis alongside a health crisis.

Whether or not we're aware of it, American Christians are baptized in the health-and-wealth gospel's false narrative. We often believe that if we are obedient and have enough faith, God will protect us from all infirmities and bless us with whatever we desire. In reality, Scripture promises no such thing.

Kate Bowler, professor of church history at Duke Divinity School and an expert on the gospel of prosperity, was diagnosed with stage-four colon cancer at age thirty. In *Everything Happens for a Reason* she writes,

> What would it mean for Christians to give up that little piece of the American Dream that says, "You are limitless"? Everything is not possible. The mighty Kingdom of God is not here yet. What if *rich* did not have to mean *wealthy*, and *whole* did not have to mean *healed*? What if being people of "the gospel" meant that we are simply people with good news? God is here. We are loved. It is enough.

As Bowler advocates, confronting false beliefs will ultimately help us to have a more integrated, grounded faith. This is crucial because long-term health issues tend to affect the spiritual (beliefs) of both the healthy spouse as well as the one who is ill. After nearly twenty years of praying for my pain to subside and asking God to help me sleep, Christopher feels weary of praying. Because I'm not fully healed, he wonders what he's doing wrong or if he should even bother to keep praying. I have repeatedly assured him that even if God does not respond the way we hope (or think he should), his prayers encourage me. And that's a good enough reason to continue.

MENTAL HEALTH ISSUES

Though the changes in our mental health are often less obvious to others, our minds, like our bodies, do not escape the effects of aging. Fluctuating hormones combined with decreased sleep, the deaths of our parents, and changing family dynamics can exceed the maximum load our psyches can bear. This may result in depression and anxiety, among other mental health issues.

Over the last twenty years, mental health practitioners have noticed a spike in depression and anxiety for all demographics. A 2009–2012 study by the Center for Disease Control found that the highest rates of depression existed for those between the ages of forty to fifty-nine, with women besting men by five percentage points (7.2 percent for men and 12.3 percent for women). Symptoms of severe depression may manifest as a diminished capacity to work, parent, and/or engage relationally; an inability to experience pleasure or find joy (known as anhedonia in clinical terms); low energy levels; trouble concentrating; and lack of interest in normal activities.

In her book *Troubled Minds*, Amy Simpson writes, "All mental illness, by definition, impairs a person's basic functioning and disrupts the kind of social connections God created us to enjoy." Writer Alia Joy, who lives with bipolar disorder, explains what those disruptions sometimes look like for her:

> In those first months on my new medications . . . I hadn't reached for my husband and was, in fact, surprised when he leaned over to kiss me and I realized I had no desire left. I hadn't even realized it had gone. It was as if that womanly part of me that used to come alive under his touch had simply vanished. . . . I pulled inward. I lost friendships. I didn't know what to say anymore. I wasn't sad so much as absent.

Like depression, anxiety has many manifestations. Anxiety is not the same as fear or worry. Simpson believes that "fear is a response to an immediate and known threat. Anxiety is a response to a possibility." That possibility, however vague or improbable, can have tremendous influence over us. Anxiety's power lies in its ability to distort reality. Anxious ruminations spin every category of thought into worst-case scenarios, particularly at night when catastrophizing or despair can easily gain the upper hand.

Based on his own struggles with anxiety, Christopher believes, "Anxiety has a watertight logic that can't be easily dissuaded. Indeed, anything may go wrong at any time, and therefore anxiety is correct that worst-case scenarios do exist. When we're flooded with anxiety, distortions rule, and we seem to overlook the little things that bring us joy and connection."

Christians don't talk about mental illness issues as openly as we need to. This can result in profound loneliness for anyone who deals with this on an ongoing basis. Though church communities shine in caring for people going through cancer treatment or when a family brings home a new baby, we can be strangely aloof in standing with individuals who experience mental illness. Unlike other areas of struggle, mental health issues carry a stigma. If we can't pray it away or count on a drug to cure it, how do we make peace with and accommodate this limitation? Because mental illness contradicts our understanding of "victorious Christian living," it's much easier for us to judge or distance ourselves from those who suffer than it is to stay close and love, particularly if there's no hope of an end date.

It's hard not to wonder if the combination of shifting hormones and the inevitable existential questions and doubts that surface during this time aren't contributing factors to the midlife spike in depression and anxiety. Upon realizing that our lives are half finished, we are compelled to reflect on our legacies. The questions and regrets can be daunting. Will our parenting mistakes affect our children for the remainder of their lives? Was it a miscalculation not to have children? Why did we wait so long to start investing in our retirement? How do I feel about the fact that I've never had the kind of professional success that I imagined or hoped for?

All of these legitimate concerns should be processed with our spouse and close friends and possibly with a therapist or spiritual director. By giving ourselves permission to ask difficult questions and reflecting on our lives up to this point, we can learn how to support each other more meaningfully.

SELF- AND SPOUSAL CARE

Unless one of us has a full-blown health crisis like Bill, we may be lulled into believing we can get away with sloppy or inconsistent self-care. The truth is, we can no longer afford to neglect our bodies. Obviously, few of us consciously choose negligence. Because there's often so much being asked of us during this season, it may be hard to prioritize or even think about taking care of ourselves.

The terminology of self-care might be part of the problem. We often associate it with getting a massage, journaling in a hip coffee shop, or binge-watching our favorite Netflix series. Self-care might include any or all those activities, but that's way too narrow. Self-care should mean creating a life that's enjoyable and sustainable for the long haul.

If we hope to be active and productive into our eighties, we need to take care of ourselves today. At a minimum, these five goals are imperative.

1. Aim to reduce the amount of sugar, processed and fried foods, and alcohol that you consume. Evidence now supports that some illnesses are linked to diet.

2. Try to get seven hours of continuous sleep each night and a minimum of forty-five minutes of exercise at least four times a week. This includes both weight bearing and cardiovascular exercises such as biking, brisk walking, jogging, or kickboxing. If you aren't currently exercising on a regular basis, start slow: aim for walking fifteen minutes every day.

3. Schedule regular checkups and screenings—especially those of you who religiously avoid such unpleasantries.

4. Create a "don't-do list." Regularly and thoughtfully evaluate what you're doing and learn how and when to say no.

5. See a professional therapist if you have any suicidal thoughts or if your depression or anxiety is affecting your daily life. Mental health issues can be addressed on many fronts, including therapy, life-style modification, and medication. While pastors and church leaders can walk with us, their expertise lies in theology, church management, and spiritual formation. Most have not been trained in physical or psychological health.

As we move through midlife, we come to understand that by taking care of ourselves, we're loving our spouse and sowing into our marriage. Though there are many aspects of the aging process that we can't control, it's prudent for us to do whatever we can to keep our bodies strong and healthy. That way, if an unexpected health crisis hits, as it did for Bill and Carol, we'll be more resourced to face it.

How did you react to the cancer discovery?

BILL   This first brush with a life-altering diagnosis was very internal. I felt like death was near but didn't want to give in to those feelings, so I leaned on God's plan being bigger than anything I could imagine or understand. At the same time, I'm still human and found myself lost in worry for my family and how this would affect them. I remember saying, *I can walk through anything, just please, God, be with them and keep them safe and in your light*. I tried to be positive and assuring. I wanted to stay strong so Carol could focus on the child growing inside her.

CAROL   In times of stress I become the logistics lady, figuring
out schedules, plans, and childcare, and Bill becomes
an outward beacon of peace. I know he was in turmoil
on the inside, but he's gifted in making those around
him think he's calm and collected! We strategized and
met with our employers; we tried to control what we
could and prayed that it would all work out.

What did life look like for the next six months?

BILL   On July 28, I had robotic surgery. On September 1, I
started the academic year with a very supportive community and was able to set up a schedule that allowed
me to work a full day and get myself to daily radiation
treatments. It was a consistent, one foot in front of the
other march. No real deep thinking. I was doing everything I could to seem like I was okay, like it was okay,
like we were okay. I wanted to disrupt our life as little
as possible and provide the opportunity for Carol to do
all the things she needed and wanted to do.

CAROL   We're both teachers, so we would get up and get out of
the house, put in full days at work, and then Bill would
head to treatment, and I would pick up our daughter
and bring her back to school with me while I finished
my duties there.

His treatment was unpleasant, to say the least. He
had second-degree burns all over his neck, lost his sense
of taste and ability to salivate, had tremendous pain,
lost his hair, choked in his sleep. This was really front
and center for everyone, including our four-year-old.

How did this affect your marriage?

BILL   This changed our entire marriage on so many levels. As the side-effects began to manifest, we drifted. I changed the way I slept—or didn't. Talking through the experience in real time was not a priority. I wanted to be encouraging during her pregnancy. In retrospect, I would recommend talking more and not assuming that your partner knows how you feel or what goes through your mind. Regarding intimacy, I wanted to be touched and connect, but between the pain of treatment and the pain of pregnancy, it was a tough season: wanting and having didn't always coincide.

CAROL   Between his treatment and my pregnancy, intimacy was hard for quite some time. That was not the only area of difficulty. I know that on some level I had become afraid of being so dependent or in love with my husband. I spent months trying to prepare for his death or disfiguration. As a result I became afraid to be vulnerable, and it's taken work to get back to a place where I'm not afraid anymore. (A year later, that work isn't over.) The threat of death just isn't sexy! I see why couples take on new roles in their marriage at some point: being a caregiver is a lot more comfortable than being the spouse preparing for a devastating loss. It's self-preservation, but it's not where we're willing to spend the remainder of our lives. So, we do the work. All the time.

How did your faith factor in?

CAROL   I was surprised at how little I felt shaken in the midst of it all. I've always been the kind of person who draws closer to God in times of turmoil and drifts in peace.

That was certainly true in this instance. In the middle of treatment I felt God embracing us every single day, and I trusted him fully. But a few months into recovery? Better yet, a year into recovery has been a slightly different story.

I don't question why God allowed this to happen, but I get angry when I think about how *forever* much of it is. I cling to the victory but am challenged daily to find peace in the little things that are gone forever. Bill breathes differently. He smells different. He's still tired. And I miss those intimate things no one else is likely to notice, and I have found myself really, really angry about losing these little things. Have I ever questioned God's love or presence or provision? No. But have I been soul-level angry with God? Resoundingly, yes.

Did this trial teach you how to love each other better or more deeply? If so, can you explain what that looked like?

BILL   It enforced that we have to work every day at understanding not only our own perspective but that of our spouse and children. Carol and I were each having different experiences during this season, which could have pushed us away from each other. We had to work to pull back together almost every day.

I've always known God's plan was bigger than I could ever understand and that worry had no value and would not change anything. As a couple we are a strong team, and we leaned on each other as we cared for our daughter, who is a force of nature. Even in a storm, our love was calm.

CAROL   I really learned what doing life with someone means. All of those vows you say at the altar that sound great are actually really difficult. To love someone and remain intimately connected to them in sickness? That doesn't just mean the flu. It means when the earth shifts under your feet, you don't run in the other direction. And the only way to do that successfully is to desperately cling to something that is bigger than the marriage itself, something that can withstand all of the earth-shifting and shattering. Doing life means being willing to part with whatever version of your relationship you are enjoying—in a split second—forever, yet remaining devoted and willing to joyfully and persistently pursue *true* spiritually nurtured and God-centered love and commitment.

Our maturing bodies constantly remind us that there's no turning back the clock to our former, younger selves. Though this is humbling and at times disempowering, it's not all bad news. The struggles and losses that are part of the aging process remind us what's important and present us with opportunities to serve, draw near to, and take comfort in each other. When viewed through this frame, our bodies become beautiful vessels containing God's grace and mercy, which we then have the privilege of pouring out on one another.

GOING DEEPER

1. How has your changing body affected your marriage, your daily life, and your intimate life? What does it look like to embrace these changes rather than fight against them?

2. If you or your spouse have any recurring or serious mental health issues (e.g., depression or anxiety), how are you addressing them?

3. What are your hopes and fears about how aging will affect your body?

4. On a scale of one to ten, how are you and your spouse taking care of yourselves? What are the barriers to good self-care? How can you and your spouse support each other in this area? What concrete changes do you need to make to help you age well?

CHAPTER FOUR

PULLED IN TWO—OR MORE—DIRECTIONS

How Midlife Caregiving Affects Marriage

S teve and Elaine's daughter, Amy, was an extremely impulsive and moody teen. Around the time she turned eighteen, things exploded overnight. Elaine describes the next season of their life:

> She became openly defiant, started staying out all night, and refused help. Not long after, she moved out and spent months couch-surfing before calling to tell us she was pregnant and getting married at the courthouse to a man she'd only known for a couple of months. I became a grandmother at age forty-four.

Five years ago Amy left her husband and two children for another man. Though she lives less than an hour away from her sons (who live with her ex), she only sees them a few times a year. She cut off almost all communication with her family. Elaine continues,

> The last decade has been exhausting in every way: physically, emotionally, spiritually, financially, and relationally. After Amy walked out on her family, I stepped in to provide childcare three days a week and on the weekends. The childcare responsibilities have limited or changed our involvement at church.

Steve and I simply couldn't participate in the same ways. We've given up social time with peers to take care of our grandsons. The grief and the weirdness of our situation have been very isolating and lonely for us.

Caregiving has many iterations in midlife, including some variations that we never expected. If we're parents, we are probably still playing an active role in our children's lives. Others of us might be involved as aunts, uncles, or grandparents. Raising children is arguably the most intense job we'll ever have. We're shaping their character, teaching them to love learning, informing their worldviews, and laying the groundwork for their own spiritual journeys. We're also refereeing, comforting, and performing thousands of seemingly mundane tasks. Children need us and they know it—even when they're teenagers. To some degree, when we choose to become a parent or guardian we understand what we're getting ourselves into and embrace what's asked of us.

Caring for an aging parent or family member is quite the opposite. Unlike our children, our mothers and fathers often resist asking for advice or practical help even when they obviously need it. "Dad, no kidding. You really shouldn't be on an extension ladder cleaning the gutters by yourself at age eighty-one." Though we understand that the final chapter in our parents' lives is coming to a close, there's no way for us to predict if they will be stricken with Alzheimer's or a stroke, thus needing years of intensive care, or if they will quietly pass away in their sleep. This ambiguity may leave us unprepared and can be quite disruptive if caregiving suddenly transitions from minor and occasional to major and ongoing.

Whether we're poised at the caregiving starting line or are approaching mile twenty-two, the unrelenting nature of simultaneously caring for children and aging family members can stress or jeopardize even the healthiest marriage. Given this reality, it's imperative for us to understand how to nurture and protect our own marriage while we serve as a solid foundation for multiple generations.

PARENTING

The demographics of marriage and parenthood in the United States have radically shifted over the past hundred years. If you're a boomer or a buster (born between 1946 and 1980), your mother probably got married in her late teens or early twenties and gave away her maternity clothes in her mid-to late thirties. Those of us who are currently over the age of forty most likely got married and started our families a bit later in life. These stats play out in my own life. My mom got married when she was twenty and had my younger sister when she was twenty-nine. I got married when I was thirty and had our third son at thirty-nine.

There are pros and cons for waiting to start a family. Women carrying children in their late thirties or early to mid-forties have an increased risk factor for complications and birth defects. As we age, our energy wanes—but, our wisdom waxes. By the time our third son came along, I was more than happy to let his brothers chase him around the playground. I may have been less involved physically, but I was more engaged emotionally and overall, a better parent. After six years on the job, I had a greater awareness of what I was getting myself into. Kind of.

None of us are ever completely prepared for parenthood. After adoption or delivery, we're handed a few essential provisions and sent away without an instruction manual. Between feeding, changing diapers, soothing colic, reducing fevers, and the heroic interventions needed to get them to sleep, it's truly miraculous that anyone decides to have more than one child. Apparently, humans have a remarkable capacity to compartmentalize pain.

Parenting turns up the heat from the refining fire that we unwittingly lit when we exchanged marriage vows. Where marriage invites us to love sacrificially, parenting demands it. This is true whether we're raising biological, step, foster, adopted, or grandchildren.

In the early years of parenting I was shocked at how frequently I felt impatient, incompetent, and angry. Looking back, I think those feelings were mostly attributable to bone-deep exhaustion, recurrent losses of control, and the lone LEGO blocks that I never saw but always stepped on. These daily humiliations became an impetus to change.

Change is essential as parents because we have to stay at least one step ahead of our offspring. This is complicated because just when we think we've got things figured out and feel some level of confidence, children catapult into another developmental stage—or, if they're teenagers, make life-altering decisions without consulting us.

How we love and care for our children as temperamental toddlers looks different when they become temperamental teenagers. Instead of waiting for their interminably long dance recitals or baseball games to end, we anxiously wait for the back door to squeak open, signaling their arrival home. We also learn how to skillfully interrogate prom dates (we might be old in their estimation, but most of us still remember our own adolescent exploits), shepherd them through their standardized tests, white-knuckle it through terrifying driving lessons, and help them imagine their tomorrows even as we support and oversee their todays.

Because teens sometimes give off the vibe that the only thing they really want from us is access to money and vehicles, we may assume that our job is mostly done and divest or even check out. In reality, they still long for and need our acceptance, affirmation, and love. Since each child matures at their own pace, we have to evaluate how to meet their needs on an ongoing, individual basis. Even though we had three sons, they all had different personalities and different needs. Despite our best attempts, we definitely did not always get it right.

From time to time the relational pushing and pulling will result in an epic battle of the wills. When it comes to discipline, giving time-outs and playing the authority card no longer work. We need to seriously up our game because they can now support their positions with nuance and logic (ish). We will be tempted to control them especially if we see them veering off (our) course. Once they hit seventeen or eighteen, this is futile. If they're losing their way, we can— and should—pray. We can reset boundaries and provide reality-based consequences. We can assure them of our love. We can do family therapy if that's appropriate. But we cannot force them to be who we want them to be. We have to learn how to respect their autonomy even if we don't agree with their decisions.

The process of relinquishing control and learning to respect is both dynamic and daunting. It's also melancholy because there's no returning to the earlier years when their neediness provided us with a clearly defined purpose and role.

The goal as parents is to work ourselves out of a job: to successfully launch our kids. Being aware of this reality does not make it any easier to let go. The love we have for our sons and daughters is powerful and profound. Next to our spouse, they know us better than anyone. They have seen us at our best and our worst. We cannot begrudge their leaving, but neither can we deny the losses that come with their departure.

It's not uncommon for these transitional phases to agitate our insecurities and widen any fissures in our marriage. Though we'd probably all agree that parenting as a united front is typically the best strategy, sometimes we're simply not on the same page. When we disagree or when the irritation that's connected to our children spills onto each other, it's easy to lose track of the presenting problem. In response we may find ourselves trying to micromanage family dynamics or unconsciously aligning with a child who is temperamentally more like us. Friends who have blended families tell me this can be particularly problematic because of the tendency to side with one's biological children.

For the most part, Christopher and I have shared big-picture parenting philosophies. We've both worked to cultivate certain character traits in our sons, including honesty, respect, gratitude, humility, and generosity. We've not always agreed on the how-tos. I'm more risk averse when it comes to physical safety. He's more courageous and empowering. He hiked down into the Grand Canyon with our oldest son as I tearfully prayed for their safe return. (If you've ever been to the Grand Canyon and read the dire warnings posted every fifty feet along the rim, you'll understand.) Navigating these differences has taught us the art of compromise.

Raising children reveals our limitations on an almost daily basis. Though uncomfortable, this is a good thing. Because we can't hide these limitations, we have to admit our frailties and ask for help. From God. From our spouse and friends. From paid professionals. Acknowledging our needs and reaching out for help increases the likelihood that our marriages will be characterized by radical love long after any children have moved on.

PARENTAL CAREGIVING 401

Though there's much overlap between caring for children and caring for aging family members, differences abound. Childhood memories hold powerful sway over our parenting philosophies. Conversely, as we care for aging family members, we stumble through uncharted territory. None of us have traveled down this road. It can be even more disorienting and pressurized than parenting because many decisions are highly consequential.

While adult children have always cared for their aging parents, shifting demographics have created an unusual plot twist: caring for multiple generations simultaneously. Author and *New York Times* columnist Jane Gross writes, "Never before have there been so many Americans over the age of eighty-five. Never before have there been so many Americans in the late middle age, the huge baby boom cohort, responsible for their parents' health and well-being." According to a study done by the Pew Research Center, 68 percent of adults between forty and fifty-nine have at least one parent aged sixty-five or older. Of that group, 55 percent provide some form of help to both a parent and one of their own children. What that help looks like will vary from family to family, but the four main types of support tend to be financial, practical, emotional, and spiritual. Each kind of support affects our marriage differently.

Any number of factors might contribute to our parents' financial stress, including escalating food, housing, and medical costs. The average monthly Social Security payment results in a well-below-poverty-line annual income of $16,848. According to financial planners, Social Security won't even cover half of retirees' needs. Hence the real and concerning gap.

Because the cost of living has outpaced the average household income, those of us who stretch to fill that gap may create our own financial insecurity. Helping our kids pay their outrageous college tuition bills and chipping in for our parents' medical or assisted-living costs can quickly deplete our often meager savings.

Offering practical support strains us in different ways. Aging seniors may require help getting dressed, clearing snow, changing light bulbs, or getting to the grocery store. Though the actual time spent serving them might be minimal, our parents' needs are often unpredictable and may conflict with the needs of our immediate family, which don't magically stop. If one of our parents has a medical emergency, as was the case with my father, life as we know it will radically and irrevocably change.

During the last week of his treatments for prostate cancer, my dad fell off the radiation table and snapped his femur. While in recovery, he went into sepsis. The doctor told me given his age and preexisting conditions, he might not survive. He did, but he never fully recovered. Thus began my immersion into adult caregiving.

My older sister and I teamed up to coordinate his care, pay his bills, and provide the encouragement he needed to get through physical therapy. More than anything else, he wanted to finish out his life in the place he called home for almost sixty years. After spending four months at the rehab center, I bundled his frail frame into my car and helped him fulfill his wish.

In addition to serving our parents' practical needs, there will be many opportunities to provide for their emotional and spiritual needs. This is often more challenging. Throughout my teen years, my father turned to alcohol to deal with his depression and combat-induced posttraumatic stress disorder. By this point in my life, I honestly believed that I was done processing the hurts connected to his choices. That perception was shattered not long after I brought him home.

My dad was not well-versed in expressing his feelings or asking for help. He had always been a proud and fiercely independent man, relying on his physical strength and engineering skills to solve life's problems. That no longer worked. I sat at his kitchen table and watched him hold back tears while the hospice worker explained possible end-of-life scenarios—all of which were bleak. A few days later he asked me to rub moisturizer on his feet. I wanted to serve him well, but such intimate contact reminded me of the times when I was a child that I longed for—but seldom received—his comfort. While I massaged the oil into his dry skin, I prayed that he would not sense my ambivalence.

As is often the case for broken parent-child relationships, healing is slow and forgiveness multilayered. I sensed that God was inviting me to love my dad regardless of his failures—or his inability to ever admit those failures—but it was much more complicated than I imagined. I ached for him to say, "I'm sorry for the ways that I hurt you." Those words never came. What does it look like for us to forgive when there's no admission of wrong? How can we give our parents the very things they were meant to give us but didn't?

Leslie Leyland Fields's book *Forgiving Our Fathers and Mothers* speaks to these questions. She writes, "In our parents' greatest hours of need, we can offer blessing instead of curses. No matter how difficult those hours are, deep moments of mercy and reconciliation can come, changing the course of *your* life, and changing the end of their lives." Her words motivated me to push through my ambivalence.

In early July of that same year, Dad's neighbor called to express his concern about my father's rapidly declining health. Christopher and I decided to make a quick trip to New Jersey in the hope of convincing him to hire a night aide. Upon our arrival, the hospice worker assured us he had a few weeks left. Intuition told us otherwise. We watched a soccer game, had dinner, and helped him settle into the hospital bed that now dominated his living room. Before he fell asleep, we prayed for him. I thanked him for being a good father and told him I loved him. And I meant it. He drew his last labored breath shortly before sunrise the next morning.

These liminal moments are holy invitations that only come around once. Until you've gone through this, it's impossible to imagine the gravity of the loss and the way it changes everything.

We will all have to say goodbye to our mothers and fathers. Even if the parent–adult-child relationship is healthy and the parent's death happens with some degree of predictability, we're seldom prepared for the avalanche of emotions triggered by this loss. My friend Ellen was in her early forties when her mom died. The two of them had worked hard for the previous twenty years to reconcile and repair their many breaches. Just when they were finally enjoying each other, Ellen lost the mother she had always longed for, which was devastating. Our parents, though imperfect, have been one of the few constants in our lives, and their departure leaves a gap that nothing and no one can fill.

THE COST OF CAREGIVING

Seeing my dad home took a toll on all of us. His sudden and unexpected transition from independent to dependent affected every aspect of our family's life for almost a year. When I was commuting across three states to care for him, I never logged in to my son's academic portals (let alone attended any parent-teacher conferences), canceled social commitments, and for the most part, abandoned Christopher. We didn't see much of each other in that season, and when we did we were always physically exhausted and one careless comment away from a fight.

The lack of sleep, discouragement, inadequate self-care, and increased responsibilities that go along with caregiving can contribute to marital discontent or even resentment. After an extended season of pouring ourselves out, we may feel like we have nothing left to offer our spouse. Even sex can become one more item on the to-do list rather than something pleasurable that unifies us.

When extreme caregiving coincides with other midlife challenges, like menopause or andropause, our grace reservoirs sometimes dry up. Behaviors we've managed to overlook for decades morph into major irritants overnight, causing us to become someone we don't recognize—and perhaps don't even like. Before menopause hit, I was the queen of multitasking. I could simultaneously make dinner, do laundry, field my son's homework questions, and cheerfully interact with my husband. Mid-menopause, God help the unsuspecting individual who asked if we had clean towels while I was scooping kibble for the dog. I also resented being the only person in the house who knew where everything was—a phenomenon I used to find amusing.

Anyone who has gone through one of these seasons will most likely not be surprised to learn that there's a bump in the divorce rate for those over the age of forty-five. Even so, the vast majority of our marriages will survive the intense seasons of parenting and caregiving. The causality of divorce is obviously complex, but one clear takeaway is that after ten, twenty, or even thirty years together, we're all vulnerable to marital discontent. As Christopher and I processed what we might have done differently during this season, we wondered if surviving was all we could expect. What would it look like to thrive when we were in the thick of it?

THRIVING VERSUS SURVIVING

A universal lesson of midlife is that we're limited people. Refusing to acknowledge this is foolish. Our bodies are no longer as nimble or strong. We may never attain the recognition or mastery in our professions that we imagined. If we accept these realities, we can become less self-oppositional and dismantle our pride (which typically impedes our growth). Humility then frees us to invite others in without triggering shame.

Coming to peace with our limitations should help us to create and maintain good boundaries. These will be organic to each marriage. Establishing and articulating clear boundaries are crucial when a high-stress task is added to one spouse's agenda. Getting specific about what we can and can't do should help our parents, children, and spouse to respect our limitations and adjust their expectations accordingly. In the last months of my father's life, I had to make it clear to Christopher and our youngest son that I would not be able to do many of the tasks that I normally shouldered. I also stepped back from all church leadership.

The goal of creating boundaries is not to shut others out and make our lives comfortable; it's to be mindful about what we can and cannot (and sometimes should not) do for others so that we can be available to do what God is asking of us. This means we'll be saying no to good opportunities and disappointing people in the process. (They'll get over it.) For recovering perfectionists like me, acknowledging that we cannot meet everyone's needs is both crushing and liberating. Earlier in my life I weathered serious shame attacks when I disappointed people. My thinking has changed. I now realize that if no one is ever disappointed with me, I probably need to reset some boundaries.

In the midst of acknowledging our limitations and setting boundaries, it's imperative that we know what we need from our spouse and then ask for it directly. That might be as simple as help making dinner or as complicated as empathy. To avoid feeling resentful, which often sneaks up on us in midlife, we need to routinely serve and sacrifice without keeping score. Marriage should never be quid pro quo. Instead, as much as we're able, we should try to out-love and out-serve each other. In *The Mystery of Marriage*, author Mike Mason refers to marriage as "a sort of contest in what might be called 'one-downmanship,' a backwards tug of war between two wills each equally determined not to win." As Steve and Elaine discovered, when both partners commit to this mindset, marriage not only eases our aloneness but also gives us resources to meet the many challenges of midlife caregiving.

Now that almost twenty years have passed, do you have clarity about what was happening with your daughter?

STEVE   Our daughter's mental health issues did not become clear to us until she left home. We had trouble with Amy during early adolescence but attributed her behavior to rebellious attitudes and bad choices. She refused the help of family and friends and was homeless at the age of eighteen.

ELAINE   She still refuses to get mental health help. We can't diagnose her, but counselors we've seen have suggested it's likely that she's dealing with bipolar, and possibly borderline personality disorder.

The demands of your life obviously did not come to a stop as you stepped in to help with her children. How did this play out?

STEVE   In the midst of all of this drama, I became unemployed for five months, we lost our home to a short sale, and Elaine was diagnosed with a rare health disorder. I've had to work through some resentment toward Amy and her refusal to parent. She's like a deadbeat parent. The emotional toll on me is heavy. It's a ride I can't get off.

ELAINE   I love my grandsons very much, but they aren't always easy to be with. We've supported them practically and formed a functional working partnership with their dad, and he and the boys often spend holidays with us. It is surreal to have an ex-son-in-law with us and our daughter basically ghosted from our lives. We've only seen her briefly in the last couple of years.

What's gotten you through this prolonged season of extreme caregiving?

STEVE   I started going to counseling to help me process my anger, loss, and grief. Prayer has been central. It's helped me to maintain focus on who is really in charge and orient me toward what I believe is most important—the goodness of God. I have reevaluated my expectations of myself and am learning to take one day at a time because there have been so many surprises (usually not good ones) in this long journey.

Elaine is amazing, strong, and wise. Marriage has provided the strength and support I've needed. I have no friends of my own who I can go to. My wife and I share friends, and we do ask them for help. Mostly,

I look for creative outlets like pottery. Elaine and I enjoy traveling and watching movies together.

ELAINE   Steve and I are really united in our commitment to one another, to God, and to our broken family. We are a team. I don't know if I'm a better spouse because of all of these challenges, but I do know we're in this together, and that's a strength and a comfort. We have both sought counseling over the last decade to process all our losses. I lost my parents during this period as well. I am hopeful as the grandsons get older and our childcare responsibilities lessen that we will be able to reclaim other parts of our lives and discover new ones together.

How have you managed not to grow bitter or resent your daughter?

ELAINE   In the early years I turned all of my blame in on myself: if I were a better mother, maybe this would not have happened. My counselor was very helpful. I never blamed Steve, and I never got the sense he blamed me. We always tried to model forgiveness with our kids and practice it with one another. In addition, we've always been a solid team in our parenting, and I think this approach kept us from blaming each other. Those habits and practices developed in our early years have sustained us during the time we've been dealing with our daughter's mental illness.

STEVE   Early on, I just went silent or exploded. Counseling helped me learn how to process those emotions. Forgiveness was always practiced.

If you had it to do over again, would you make the same choices about stepping in to care for your grandsons?

ELAINE   If we had to do it over again, I'd back up the script to the point when our daughter first began exhibiting signs of mental illness and be more aggressive about seeking help for her. We chalked so much of it up to mercurial teen mood swings. While both of those played a role, she needed professional help, and we didn't recognize it until after when she was a legal adult. That decision could have changed the trajectory of her life and the experience our grandkids have had. Still, I remain grateful for the time we've had with them. I love them very much.

STEVE   Stepping in to care for the grandsons seemed like the compassionate thing to do. We had a choice. We could have turned away because when you get down to it, to some extent we are filling in for a mother who chose to abandon her children. Why should we take any responsibility for her choices? But that seemed insensitive.

How did the two of you stay connected in these difficult years?

STEVE   All that we've gone through together has made us a stronger and better team. Is it all rosy now? No. We still have challenges ahead of us like relocation, my aging parents (both in their mid-to late eighties), and possibly having to care for them. We are going through hell or high water together, with God at our side.

ELAINE   When we got married, I remember imagining I was now in a room with no doors but with an open roof. I was going to need to remain committed to being in that room, not looking for a way to climb out of the marriage when things got hard. Despite all of the changes and challenges, we're in the room together. Now we have a long history and are committed to future growth. That history and the freedom to continue to grow binds us together until death parts us.

⤙⤚

Caring for children and family members is equally sacred and taxing. Perhaps the only way we can generously, faithfully serve multiple generations *and* nurture our marriage is by relying on a source outside of ourselves who is unlimited and who will never fail or forsake us. That would be Jesus.

GOING DEEPER

1. How have the demands of parenting or taking care of family members affected your marriage? Be specific. What's been a blessing? What's been more difficult than you imagined?

2. How has your intimate life been affected by taking care of others? How could you and your spouse move toward each other in this season?

3. How do you feel about being limited? How easy or difficult is it for you to admit your limitations and ask for help? How could God use these limitations to help you receive love and grace from your spouse and friends?

4. If you and your spouse do not share the same parenting philosophies or goals, how does that affect your marriage and your children? How could you find common ground?

CHAPTER FIVE

DECIPHERING DISAPPOINTMENT

The Road to Contentment

M ark and Isabella got married a mere six months after they met. The next day they drove more than a thousand miles across three states for Mark's new job. On Monday he walked out the door for work, leaving her home alone in a community where they had no friends or family. Isabella was twenty.

She recounts:

That was the most difficult year of my life. We didn't even really know each other. We were apart for most of our engagement. Once we were married, when he came home from work, he was exhausted and just wanted to play video games.

Prior to our wedding I had already experienced quite a few disappointments. Weeks before I was supposed to start college, my parents told me they couldn't afford for me to go. Come September, instead of being away at school, I was working, going to community college, and living at home, needing to obey my parents' curfew. When I asked if I could move out on my own, my father told me, "The only way you can move out of this house is if you get married."

Mark pursued me hard. He was a Christian. He wanted to be a pastor. I was just checking off the boxes and seeing all that we had in common. I didn't think about how our personalities and our families of origin would make such a huge difference. His parents divorced when he was very young. My family was intact. I saw what my parents had and knew what the fairy tales said and thought, *That's how it's going to work.* Our reality was different.

I'm very romantic and idealistic. Mark was a pragmatist. Because we were so different and because he had a somewhat traumatic childhood, he was not able to meet my emotional or relational needs. We promised each other that divorce wasn't an option, but I had no one to talk to and didn't know what to do with my disappointment.

Though Isabella's disappointment lasted the entirety of her marriage, she did not leave Mark. Staying with him was possible because of the strength and comfort she received from Jesus. In fact, enduring hardship in the company of Christ is part of what made her into the remarkable, resilient woman she is today.

How we respond to disappointments can make or break our marriage. If we fail to address them, disappointments can accumulate and morph into disillusionment, despair, and resentment. For this complicated feeling to have any payoff, we must not view it as an inconvenience or irritation but as an invitation to grow. By accepting this invitation, we can learn to whole-heartedly love our spouse without needing them to become someone else.

DISAPPOINTMENT'S DNA

Disappointment has many faces which makes it difficult to identify. I asked my Facebook friends to describe how they feel or react when disappointed. It was my most commented-on post ever. Responses included sadness, frustration, anger, guilt, shame, blame, binge watching, and self-medicating (e.g., eating or drinking too much). Because of its complexity, it has taken Christopher and me decades to recognize and address some of our marital disappointments. He had the following epiphany only a few years ago:

> I used to believe that men come into marriage with fewer expectations than women do, but I have begun to question that conclusion. I now understand that I've experienced disappointment in our marriage connected to three areas: food, chores, and emotional availability.
>
> I come from an Italian American family. The quantity of food was every bit as important as the quality. Because our extended family all lived in the area and we never knew who might opportunistically drop by at mealtime, my mother always made infinitely more than the five of us could ever eat. Dorothy hates to waste food. Early on I felt frustrated with her for not catering to my expectations and cooking copious amounts of everything.
>
> I know the division of labor is a common area of conflict for many couples, and we're no different. I grew up with a magic hamper. I could wear something once, drop it in the hamper, and find it ironed and hanging in my closet or folded and put away when I came home from school. Dorothy did not grow up with a magic hamper and we did not receive one as a shower gift. Needless to say, that's not how doing laundry has worked in our marriage.
>
> Regarding emotional availability, I'm a four on the Enneagram, which means I need others to notice my specialness. I'm sure that's part of what propelled me into theater. I'm totally extroverted and use more words than the average male. Being listened to helps me feel loved. Dorothy is a good listener, but

there's no way that she can satisfy my need to be heard. If she did, she'd never get any work done when I'm home. I can understand how my expectations are unrealistic, but I still feel let down when she indicates I've reached my word quota for the day.

Despite my deep love and profound respect for Christopher, I've had my own disappointments. Unbeknownst to me, I walked down the aisle carrying specific expectations for him, most notably *how* he should express love and affirmation. I wanted the perfect gift on special occasions. I wanted to hear him say, "You look beautiful!" or "That might be the best talk you've ever given!" more than once a year. Unfortunately, Christopher's family has a complex relationship with gift giving and affirmation. Gifts were seldom chosen with the recipient in mind, leaving him and his siblings feeling perplexed and unknown. If his mom cooked a delicious meal, his dad would offer this rather obtuse praise: "It came good." Knowing his family put his behavior in perspective, but it didn't eradicate my disappointment. When I looked beautiful or nailed a talk and he was silent, my disappointment turned to hurt and sometimes anger.

THE DISAPPOINTMENT-EXPECTATION CONNECTION

Most of our disappointments can be traced directly back to our expectations. Every one of us brings multiple expectations into marriage. Some of those expectations include fidelity, honesty, and sexual intimacy—all essential components for healthy marriages. But here's the rub: we tend to be specific about how our spouse should meet these desires. In other words, we have expectations about our expectations. Christopher and I each expected love on our terms, and those terms were not congruent.

Given the link between expectations and disappointment, you might assume that if you jettison the former, you'll avoid the latter. Because expectations reference our wants and needs, we're better off paying attention to rather than ignoring them. Then as we gain clarity, we can negotiate and, when necessary, recalibrate. Understanding where our expectations come from can help us to sort this out. I'd like to suggest three possible sources: our family of origin, the culture at large, and our historic wounds.

Family of origin. Though we are largely oblivious to this reality, while growing up, our family of origin influences everything from our taste buds to our vacation preferences to our political leanings to how we deal with (or avoid) conflict. Developmental experts agree children learn by watching and copying those around them. They quickly understand which emotions elicit rewards (namely, praise and inclusion) and which ones lead to rejection or punishment. Children learn to be part of the whole by fitting in rather than deviating from family norms. If we value our family and our culture, we tend to conform to the same patterns and behaviors. When we dislike or disapprove of our familial and cultural norms, we tend to break away and establish new patterns and behaviors.

If your family always went on vacation, it's hardwired into your psyche to retrieve the suitcases from the attic every July. Again, most expectations are not vague or generalized. We have specific expectations formed through specific experiences. If you stayed in five-star hotels on the beach, a Motel 6 along an interstate highway is probably not going to cut it. If your spouse's childhood birthdays included cards, gifts, and special meals, grabbing a bunch of dyed carnations and a sappy card from the grocery store will probably fall short of their expectations.

Some of our family-based expectations are gender specific. For many of us who grew up in the sixties or seventies, there was a neat—albeit inequitable—division of domestic labor. Fathers earned money, mowed the lawn, maintained the car, and barbecued. Mothers were often responsible for everything else—even if they worked outside the home.

My dad loved taking care of our cars. He faithfully and proactively rotated the tires, replaced the wiper blades, and changed the oil in my '72 Chevy without me ever needing to ask him. Though I never communicated this expectation to Christopher, I definitely assumed he would eagerly and cheerfully do the same. In turn, he believed that I would be delighted to wash and iron his clothes, in part because his mom took such pride in this chore. We both came into marriage wanting to transcend our parents' beliefs about gender roles, but instead we fell into familiar patterns.

To make matters worse, we moralized our perspectives. Christopher felt I *should* want to do his laundry, and I believed he *should* take care of our car. When we attach moral energy to our way of moving through life, it naturally leads to judgment, which often results in conflict. In my worldview timeliness is a virtue. Christopher is a time optimist. He sees time as a metaphor. *Now* means something different to each of us. No surprise, we've had our share of heated conversations about what it means to be on time for everything from dinner to doctors' appointments.

The two of us have also had conflict about conflict. His Italian American family thought nothing of yelling at each other when they were angry. My northern European family defaulted to silence and stiff upper lips. Early on in our marriage when his vocal volume exceeded what I believe to be a normal decibel level, I assumed he was furious and pleaded with him to dial down. He wasn't furious: that's what engagement looked like in his household.

Provided that our spouse's practices and beliefs do not conflict with the gospel or dishonor us, we should endeavor to respect cultural differences rather than dismiss them or try to convince our spouse to be more like us. After all, we are supposed to conform to the image of Christ—not each other.

Cultural landscape. The dominant culture (both secular and religious) where we spent our formative years also deeply affects us. To grow up in the United States is to be influenced by American values such as individualism, optimism, and ownership. These values shape our decision making and our expectations for what every-day life is supposed to look like.

The prevailing culture also informs our expectations for relationships: particularly romantic ones. As a child of the sixties, I watched every Disney movie ever made and grew up scanning the horizon for a prince riding a white horse whose kiss had the power to break evil spells. Christopher is an amazing lover, a faithful husband, and a determined provider. However, he has no blue blood, no equestrian abilities, and his kisses have not healed me of my infirmities. Disney movies have evolved, but back then, the heroes and heroines adhered to strict gender norms. The heroes got to do all the fun stuff. The heroines spent a lot of time cleaning, singing, and waiting. I don't particularly enjoy any of those activities. And truth be told, Christopher is actually much better at cleaning and singing than me. (Neither of us are good at waiting.) By this point in our marriage, we no longer feel limited by culturally-bound gender norms. Early on, we embraced what we knew.

Those who hold some type of religious affiliation will have additional expectations to sift through. Many of the expectations rooted in Judeo-Christian beliefs are inarguably good and beneficial for marriage (e.g., fidelity, forgiveness, and sobriety). But religiously based expectations can land in the negative column, particularly when cultural traditions become religious mandates.

For example, certain strains of Christianity expect women to not only prioritize homeschooling but also forsake any professional endeavors outside the home. I believe that families should have the freedom to follow their convictions. And in full disclosure, we taught our sons at home for ten years. That said, in many believing households, both parents need to work to make ends meet, which eliminates the option of homeschooling. Furthermore, the concept of mothers focusing their energies solely on raising and schooling their children is a product of modern culture, not Scripture, as the Proverbs 31 wife demonstrates.

Pain. The third influencer of our expectations is connected to our historic wounds. Humans are wired to detect and withdraw from things that hurt us. That's why our hand reflexively drops a hot pan before we're even aware of what we're doing. Muscle memory helps us to avoid making the same mistake. Likewise, our psyches, which remember emotional and relational hurts, try to protect us by informing our expectations for each other.

Christopher can trace his expectations for me to endlessly listen back to a dysfunctional family dynamic. The Grecos' operatic style of talking over each other while exchanging verbal jabs resulted in lots of laughs and, at least for him, profound loneliness. Being heard is one of the primary ways we feel known. Christopher did not feel known or understood by his family, which was deeply painful. I can trace my heightened desire for affirmation directly to my childhood. I was a highly sensitive and incredibly shy child who was often misunderstood and teased. I expected Christopher to compensate for my insecurities by peeling off the old labels and affirming me.

All expectations need to be assessed with discernment and care. Because they're often formed subconsciously and tend to be deeply embedded, it's not always easy for us to identify them, let alone understand how they affect our spouse. By learning to recognize and then evaluate our expectations for each other and for our marriage, we'll experience less disappointment and greater marital satisfaction.

THE HIDDEN PROMISE OF DISAPPOINTMENT

Disappointment can help us become more content and more accepting if we discern what it's trying to teach us. If we ignore disappointment's message, we may short-circuit the process of transformation that midlife means to impart.

Disappointments expose the limits of our power. I cannot make Christopher notice that I look beautiful or force complimentary words out of his mouth. Likewise, no matter how much he longs for me to be like him, he cannot make me an external processor. Once we realize and accept the limits of our power, it should allow us to refocus our energies on what we can change.

The reality is we aren't powerless, but we only have the authority to change ourselves, and even that is limited when it comes to certain issues. If we focus on how the other person needs to change—and plot how that's going to happen—we will probably get stuck in disappointment or possibly descend into disillusionment or despair.

Disappointments also give us opportunities to discern if we have any disordered desires (see chapter 2). When Christopher links his worth to how engaged the congregants are during worship, he's going to feel disappointed and insecure when many of them are checking their social media feeds. When I expect Christopher to tell me who I am rather than going to God for my identity, I'm going to feel disappointed and hurt when he does not comply with my agenda. Christopher can affirm my identity, but God is the only one who can name me. When we expect our spouse to fill God's role, we will inevitably feel disappointed. Disordered desires wreak havoc on all relationships. Particularly marriage. Again, the solution is not to cut ourselves off from desire but to rightly order those desires.

Finally, confronting our disappointments helps us to move toward loving our spouse for who they are, not who we think they should be. There's a reciprocal nature to this. We love our spouses despite their limitations and weaknesses and, in turn, hope that they will likewise love us. If you're uncertain about whether or not you're holding unrealistic expectations for your spouse or your marriage, pay attention to places where you overreact, have routine conflict, or judge each other. You could also ask a variation of this question: How realistic are my expectations based on who I married? Not who I think I married, not who I hoped to marry, but who I actually married.

My desire for Christopher to regularly affirm me is not wrong, but it is unrealistic based on who he is. Neither is it wrong for him to want me to listen as he processes his many thoughts. Our desires for our spouse do not magically empower them to become a different version of themselves. If you're married to someone who is clinically depressed or on the spectrum, it's possible that some of the expectations you brought into marriage will need to be renegotiated. (More on this shortly.)

It's helpful to have ongoing, nondefensive conversations where we can parse out our wants, needs, and expectations. This is one of the most difficult yet most essential opportunities of midlife marriage. If we continue to cling to our unrealistic expectations, we not only become entrenched and inflexible but are also in danger of becoming bitter and resentful. Conversely, as we begin to form healthy, realistic expectations, it frees us to fully embrace our spouse because we're no longer judging them or needing them to be someone else.

By digging into his disappointments, Christopher was able to discern which ones were unrealistic or selfish. Those realizations provided traction to change.

Dorothy may not make as much food as I think she should, but the quality is better than I could ever pull off. I've learned to turn my expectations about mealtime into appreciation for her.

With regard to my expectations about laundry, I can turn my disappointment into personal action. Rather than expecting her to iron my shirts or track what should or shouldn't go into the dryer, I can do it myself. I'm an adult after all.

Letting go of my expectations about her listening to me has been more difficult. Because of my temperament and my sin patterns, I have to push myself to remember that Dorothy has had her own experience during the last twelve hours and is an introvert to boot. Nary a week goes by when I have no memory of a conversation we had. I now see the double standard: I want her to listen to me, but I don't have to listen to her. Here, I can turn my disappointment into repentance.

In other words, relational disappointment can provide opportunities for us to show gratitude, take positive action, and repent of our sin. That's good news.

The fact that our disappointments can expose our sin is one of their greatest gifts to us. We believe ourselves to be kind, selfless, reasonable people. If there's anybody in the world who sees our self-deception, it's our spouse. That sobering reality is not meant to crush us but to motivate us to move toward Christ and toward transformation.

As you'll read in the interview with Isabella, this process is infinitely more complicated if one spouse wants to grow but the other does not feel the need or desire to change.

⌐❀¬

Thinking back over the course of your marriage, do you think Mark felt any of the same disappointment that you did?

ISABELLA   He didn't. When I asked him during those early years, he said, "I'm not beating you or being unfaithful, so what's wrong? We're fine."

So he did not have the same standard for a good marriage?

ISABELLA   No, he did not. I'd ask him if we could go to marriage counseling, and he'd say, "That's for people who are having a hard time." He knew I wasn't happy, but he was content.

How did you make it through those early years?

ISABELLA I just kept busy. I went back to school during the day and worked a part-time job at night. Eventually, I got my nursing license, and then we had our first child. That baby filled a void for me. She was someone to love, and she loved me back.

Meanwhile, all this time you still carried a long-term desire to do missions work. Did that ever become part of your married life?

ISABELLA We did a short-term project, and then a few years later God opened up an opportunity for us to become full-time missionaries in South America. I'm a native Spanish speaker, and Mark was not. That meant I had to do all of the translating work, and we didn't always agree on how to minister, which caused tension. No one else spoke English in the area where we lived. After two weeks of going to a Spanish-speaking church, Mark said, "I'm done. I can't go to this church anymore." So I went alone, which was another disappointment.

From the outside, it looked like I was finally living my dream. After all, I'm doing missions work with my husband. At some point I realized I needed to stop focusing on the negative. But I still had no one to connect with and no place to unload my heart.

(After serving in South America for a number of years, Mark was called to the pastorate, and the family returned to the States. Isabella and Mark had the chance to return to South America on a short-term mission trip a few years later. When she was flying home, Isabella inexplicably started weeping. The tears kept flowing all summer.)

What was going on for you in that season?

ISABELLA   I just couldn't stop crying. I wondered what was wrong with me. I had a nice house, healthy kids, a husband who was in ministry. I could see no reason to be sad. I forced myself to get up in the morning, made sure the kids were taken care of, and got them to school, but then I just wanted to crawl back to bed. I was finally diagnosed with depression. Though I was initially resistant, I started taking medication, which helped almost immediately.

A few years later, Mark was diagnosed with an aggressive form of cancer. How did his illness affect your marriage?

ISABELLA   For most of my married life I felt like I was at the edge of a lake picking up pebbles, naming each one with the disappointments I had experienced and then throwing them into the center of the lake. When Mark got sick, it was as if this big boulder called cancer fell into the lake and all of the pebbles rose to the top. I felt like God said to me, "You need to deal with all of the things you've submerged for all these years." I thought, *My husband is fighting for his life. I don't think this is the time for me to bring up all the hurts and disappointments.*

I went to see a marriage counselor and told her what was going on. She encouraged me to tell him in the hope that we could end well. I asked Mark if we could talk about it. He had not been open to hearing it before. For the first time he was able to admit that he struggled with being emotionally intimate. But he also communicated that he was not able to work on changing. At that time I shut down. I knew I wasn't going to walk away from him as he was dying, but I also felt I could not endure any more pain.

(Isabella and Mark were married for more than twenty years when he passed away. After he died, there were days when she went in to work, closed the office door, and wept. Five years after Mark's death, she went on a retreat hoping to find more healing.) How did you deal with your disappointment and grief?

ISABELLA I had so much hurt. Not being able to go to that Christian college, marriage not being what I imagined, Mark's illness and death, having to raise my kids alone. During this time away, I was finally able to express my anger with God. The spiritual director gave me boxing gloves and led me to a punching bag. She said, "You're not allowed to walk away until you've communicated all of your feelings to God." I was there for a long time.

Proverbs says, "A man makes his plans but the LORD directs his steps." During the retreat, I felt like God asked me, "You planned a certain life, but it didn't quite work out as you thought it would. Will you trust me?" I have to be able to say, "Of course, I trust you." If I look back and see all that God has done, I see his goodness and his provision. I see our amazing children growing into wonderful young adults. I remember how God pulled me out of the pit of depression. I have no idea what the future holds, but I trust that he will be with me and sustain me just as he has done for my entire life.

(Isabella was single for six years after Mark died. She recently remarried and is thrilled to have a second chance. Isabella knows that she will still experience disappointment from time to time, but she now feels better equipped to deal with it. Because she faithfully processed her pain and disappointment, she was ready to risk loving again.)

All of us will occasionally ride waves of disappointment in our marriages. This does not indicate that we're incompatible. Disappointment becomes problematic when we perceive ourselves to be victims, blame our spouse, or fail to grow.

It took Christopher and me almost twenty years to excavate our disappointments. Now that we've (mostly) let go of our unrealistic expectations and (mostly) figured out how to extend grace and mercy to each other when we feel disappointment, we have fewer conflicts and more energy to authentically love each other. That translates to a much more fulfilling and joyful marriage.

GOING DEEPER

1. How do you respond/react when you are disappointed?

2. If you traced your marital disappointments backward, what would you discover? Do you recognize and can you articulate the expectations that you have for your spouse and for your marriage? What would it look like to have honest, vulnerable conversations with your spouse about your expectations and disappointments?

3. What would it feel like to admit that even if your marriage is good and enjoyable, it's not everything you hoped for or imagined? If you've intuited that it's better not to go there, what's the cost of avoidance?

4. How do your limitations affect your spouse? How do they affect your marriage?

5. If there are any places in your marriage or your life where disappointment has morphed into discouragement, despair, or resentment, how could you begin to address this?

CHAPTER SIX

NAVIGATING TRAUMA AND LOSS

The Real Crises

One seemingly normal summer day, Katherine and Rick received a frantic phone call informing them that their son was in respiratory failure. They raced to his friend's house in time to witness paramedics performing CPR as they moved him into the waiting ambulance. Miraculously, he survived. Then their nightmare began.

Unbeknownst to them, their son had become addicted to heroin. Katherine explains,

> At the time, neither my husband nor I knew much about drugs, so when we first saw our son—intubated, unconscious, and barely alive—a whole new, ugly world suddenly opened up to us. Our stable, do-this-and-all-will-be-well lives spun into fear, confusion, and desperation. From that first day when he overdosed, it would be years before we would be able to sleep through the night and not freak out every time the phone rang.

Crises of this magnitude can contribute to the demise of a marriage —or help it to grow stronger. What makes the difference? As Rick and Katherine's story demonstrates, though trauma and loss can make us feel like powerless victims, they do not strip us of our agency. We get to choose how we respond. If we commit to loving and supporting each other, even on the darkest days, and refuse to let the crisis divide us, our marriages will increasingly become places of refuge and sources of strength. For us and for everyone around us.

TRAUMA'S LONG LEGACY

Trauma is an emotional or physical wound that has long-lasting consequences. The effects might be evident, such as a broken leg due to a car crash, or invisible to everyone except the survivor, such as nightmares, panic attacks, angry outbursts, or severe depression. In her seminal book *Trauma and Recovery*, Dr. Judith Herman explains that "traumatic events generally involve threats to life or bodily integrity, or a close personal encounter with violence and death. They confront human beings with the extremities of helplessness and terror, and evoke the responses of catastrophe."

We tend to associate trauma with violent crime or warfare and therefore believe that it primarily affects rape victims, military personnel, and first responders (e.g., paramedics and police officers). The truth is, many of us carry trauma-related wounds.

Statistics show that in the United States, one in four children are physically abused, one in three couples have been physically violent with one another, one in four of us grew up with an alcoholic in the family, and one in three women and one in six men will experience some form of sexualized violence. Being in a serious accident, witnessing a violent crime, losing a home in a natural disaster, having a child go through a medical emergency, getting divorced (or watching your parents divorce as a child), and being exposed to pornography at a young age can all register as trauma. Unfortunately, few studies or statistics include racialized trauma, which occurs on an ongoing basis and deeply affects people of color.

It's not a question of *if* you or your spouse have experienced trauma. It's more a question of *to what degree* and *have the two of you ever considered how past trauma might be affecting your marriage today.*

The chronology of trauma awareness and treatment is important. The social revolution of the 1960s (particularly as it pertained to a growing awareness of violence against women) coupled with the return of Vietnam veterans pushed the psychiatric and medical community to broaden their understanding of trauma and offer more comprehensive treatment options. That said, posttraumatic stress disorder (PTSD) didn't get included into the American Psychiatric Association's Diagnostic and Statistical Manual (known as the DSM) until 1980, and it wasn't until the late 1990s (after the Adverse Childhood Experiences Study was published) that trauma diagnosis and therapy became more mainstream. Because of this lag, anyone over the age of fifty who experienced early trauma may have suffered silently, been blamed for their struggles, or worse, been accused of being morally weak. Research now supports that the effects of trauma are far reaching and pernicious.

When a traumatic event happens to us, there's a ripple effect. Trauma affects the entire brain, particularly the amygdala and the hippocampus, which are both part of the limbic system. (The limbic system is often referred to as the emotional brain.) Trauma leads to either hyperarousal (i.e., always on high alert) or hypoarousal (i.e., shut down). The term *dissociation* refers to a person's ability to split off from these traumatic experiences, only to be overpowered during uncontrollable flashbacks or in response to unexpected or seemingly random triggers. Some individuals who face unresolved, complex trauma (e.g., child abuse) can live in a constant state of partial dissociation: physically present but emotionally absent. Needless to say, that makes for unsatisfying relationships.

After a traumatic event, the prefrontal cortex (the rational brain) tries to make sense of what happened. Because trauma doesn't make sense, the prefrontal cortex ends up being in conflict with the limbic system. When stressed or threatened, even if it's a minor or insignificant threat, the limbic system can override the prefrontal and the medial prefrontal cortex, causing trauma victims to respond in ways that may be completely irrational or totally out of character.

Christopher has vivid boyhood memories of his father's explosive rage, which included spanking with a leather belt and embarrassing public outbursts with voice-cracking profanity. His father would express remorse and shame after blowing up, but the outbursts persisted, often when least expected. Even into his early thirties, if anyone—even me—unexpectedly touched Christopher from behind, he not only had a startle response but also would react with anger and then be overcome with shame. It's only in midlife that Christopher and his siblings have become aware of how damaging their father's behavior was.

After a traumatic event has ended, the body continues to secrete stress hormones keeping victims ready to respond to the next threat. If unaddressed, this can result in health issues such as depression, cardiovascular disease, or digestive issues. Trauma is not simply psychological; our bodies continue to react until we have processed the trauma and feel some sense of safety and control.

The long-term effects of trauma depend on many variables, including our personalities, when the trauma happened (the earlier in life, the more severe), whether or not we have a trauma history (Is this the first or the tenth trauma we've endured?), and how those closest to us responded (Was it ignored or appropriately addressed?). Someone who grew up in a healthy, well-boundaried family, and sailed through adolescence and early adulthood with nary a scrape might be able to face the 2020 pandemic with confidence and hope. In contrast, someone else who experienced childhood trauma and then later battled cancer or worked at ground zero on 9/11 might experience panic attacks or other PTSD symptoms and descend into catastrophic thinking as the coronavirus death toll rises.

Because of how and where traumatic memories are stored in the brain, it can be difficult to access and talk about traumatic events. This is why certain types of therapy, such as eye movement desensitization and reprocessing (EMDR), can be more successful than traditional talk therapy for some individuals.

Traumatic experiences are always adverse and should never be ignored or dismissed. Processing trauma with a professional therapist (particularly one who specializes in this type of work) while in a healthy, safe marriage will enhance the healing process. In fact, intimate relationships where the survivor feels safe and can reestablish autonomy and a sense of self-control are essential components of recovery.

As we do our work, wounds will heal, providing opportunities to connect more consistently, trust more fully, and find freedom from trauma's grip. This kind of healing allows us to be more resilient, which is important because of the many losses that we face in the middle of our lives.

MIDLIFE LOSSES

Losses occur at any—and every—stage of life, but once we enter our fourth decade, they begin to accumulate. In *Life Reimagined*, Barbara Bradley Hagerty laments that

> troubles start to cluster at midlife: You are more likely to lose a parent or spouse after forty, more likely to be diagnosed with cancer after forty-five, and much more likely to be replaced by a younger, cheaper, more tech-savvy employee after fifty. I never gave much thought to rebounding from setbacks in my twenties or thirties, because life was ascendant and setbacks were rare. Now I feel as if I spend half my time trying to plug leaks in the dam.

Hagerty might be waxing hyperbolic, but then again some weeks I feel like all I do is mop up leaks.

In addition to the loss of significant relationships (see chapter 4), perhaps the most common midlife losses occur in the following three categories: roles, trust, and faith.

Loss of roles. Between the ages of forty and sixty-five, our roles—how we understand ourselves in relationship to others and to the world around us—shift significantly.

If our primary focus for the past two or three decades has been caring for and nurturing family members, we may feel adrift after our parents pass away and our kids move on. When the roles that have defined us change, it can leave us feeling invisible, angry, regretful, and scrambling to repurpose our skills, or wondering if we've "passed our expiration date." How do we convince potential employers that the skills we've been honing—including managing complex schedules, resolving seemingly intractable conflicts, and staying on budget—make us exceedingly competent for many types of work? It would seem that potential employers should be fighting over us. Sadly, that's typically not what happens.

Due to rapid technological advances, certain jobs have changed so drastically that we may no longer be qualified. One fifty-something friend who is an architect by trade is finding it almost impossible to reenter the workforce at her previous level of expertise. She explains,

> While I was raising my four children, architecture transitioned to computer-aided design. Firms are now looking for employees who are inexpensive but already proficient. I've wondered if I should just give up on my profession or retool in a completely new direction. Though I know I have much to contribute, this uncertainty causes me to question myself and my abilities.

This dilemma might be more common for women because, statistically, we are more likely to be the primary caregivers. But men can also experience a similar disequilibrium as they age. Since our culture is so enamored with youth, many men in their fifties and sixties feel pressure to prove their competence in the workplace or risk being pushed out. Gone are the days when men could find a stable job in their twenties, steadily advance, and comfortably retire in their early sixties.

On the plus side, professional and relational losses can provide us with opportunities to reevaluate our lives and potentially do something new that's equally or perhaps even more meaningful. By paying close attention to the effects of these role shifts, we can support each other and ease the internal chaos that we often experience in seasons of uncertainty.

Loss of trust. When I bring up the loss of trust in the context of marriage, some might immediately associate that with adultery or other highly consequential moral failures. But the loss of trust doesn't happen only when we discover that our spouse has been having an affair or that their monthly massage included a "happy ending."

Being married to someone who has stellar intentions but limited capacity or willpower to follow through can also register as a loss of trust. When our spouse promises to curb their spending, cut back on consuming alcohol, or work fewer hours but repeatedly fails, it's frighteningly easy to become cynical or resentful.

If your spouse has been unfaithful or has engaged in a serious moral transgression, you might immediately be plunged into a crisis, the severity of which depends on many variables. Did your spouse out themselves, or did you discover the affair when they inadvertently left their iPad at home? Are they willing to immediately stop seeing their lover and start couples' counseling, or are they defensive and recalcitrant?

Regardless of whether you're dealing with a full-blown affair, sporadic hook-ups, or online cheating, violations of trust are perhaps the most painful and devastating crises a married couple will ever face. When two adults have promised to forsake all others until they are separated by death and one party reneges, the wound is jagged and bloody. And if it happened once, what's to say it won't happen again? Trust can be regained, but it will not be quick or easy, and it's up to the betrayer to rebuild that trust. That means, among other things, ruthless honesty, sharing computer logins with accountability partners, giving each other unlimited phone access, going to counseling, and attending a recovery group.

Loss of trust is also a factor when emotional or physical abuse has taken place. The shame and secrecy that are part of an abusive system make it difficult to reach out for help. Approximately ten million men and women will be physically abused by an intimate partner every year in the United States alone. Abuse often begins subtly and worsens incrementally. One partner may limit access to finances, make all or most of the consequential decisions, and then begin to belittle and isolate the victimized spouse from friends and family. When physical violence follows, the victim can feel like they deserve it because that's the message they have been receiving for years. Far too often, Christian women on the receiving end of abuse are counseled to stay with their spouse and pray. This is unhelpful, misguided, and potentially dangerous. If you are being abused by your spouse, please seek help. There is a list of resources in the appendix.

Ongoing abuse within marriage is one of several legitimate reasons to explore separation or divorce. Even though divorce is more common today than it was in 1969 when California became the first state to legalize no-fault divorce, there's still a stigma attached to it in many Christian circles. Those of us on the outside must remember that it's perhaps the most agonizing decision anyone will ever make. Better for us to stand with and love our friends as they explore whether or not their marriage can be saved than to judge them or offer overly simplistic advice. One friend recalled how deeply moved she was when, in the midst of moving toward divorce, someone stopped by her workplace with a cup of tea and a muffin and simply said, "I felt like I was supposed to bring this to you today." These small gestures of kindness can be lifelines to men and women as they navigate the heartbreak of divorce.

Loss of faith. It's no surprise that the cumulative effect of disappointment, grief, trauma, and loss sometimes causes our faith to shift. Christopher and I did not have a marital crisis during our year from hell, but we certainly both experienced a crisis of faith that profoundly affected our marriage.

In this season we went from feeling confident about our ability to hear from God to wondering whether hearing from God was even possible. It was as if we lost our Wi-Fi connection mid-conversation. Our doubts and uncertainties became like static, drowning out God's voice.

In the New Testament, Jesus likens himself to a shepherd and we are his sheep. We are meant to follow him by learning how to distinguish his voice from others that might lead us astray. Without his voice we can feel abandoned and confused. This is not to devalue or dismiss the importance of turning to Scripture, particularly as we make consequential decisions. God's Word, along with the counsel of trusted friends, can guide and encourage us. But for those of us who have come to rely on God's presence in prayer or worship, silence can be disorienting and disturbing.

Throughout history, many men and women have spent years, sometimes even decades, straining to hear God's voice or trying to understand the purpose of his seeming silence. According to her posthumously released letters, Mother Teresa felt abandoned by God for more than fifty years. She was forty-nine when she wrote, "If I ever become a saint—I will surely be one of darkness."

Author and activist Marlena Graves has personally experienced what is often referred to as the dark night of the soul. She has come to believe that

God uses the desert of the soul—our suffering and difficulties, our pain, our dark nights (call them what you will)—to form us, to make us beautiful souls. He redeems what we might deem our living hells, if we allow him. The hard truth, then, is this: Everyone who follows Jesus is eventually called into the desert.

Being called into the desert often includes being blasted with sandstorms of doubt and disillusionment. Where do we turn when the Scripture no longer offers comfort, when our prayers feel like little more than superstitious chants, or when cynicism swallows up hope? Christopher explains how our crisis affected him spiritually:

> I felt as if God flipped the chess board and said, "New game," while I argued, "I know it's a stalemate but let me keep playing." To make meaning out of our losses, I endlessly replayed events and rehearsed contingencies. I identified with Orual in C. S. Lewis's *Till We Have Faces*, who poured out her complaint "over and over . . . I would have read it forever, quick as I could, starting the first word again almost before the last was out of my mouth, if the judge had not stopped me."
>
> Fears of future calamity pervaded my thinking, and it took about three years to stop looking over my shoulder for something worse to befall us. It's also true that I landed on my feet vocationally, and there I was, leading hundreds of people in worship week after week, and meaning it. I didn't know I could experience such tearing and such resilience simultaneously.

I've been following Jesus for more than forty years. In my twenties and thirties, it was common for me to feel disappointed or angry at God when hardship came my way, particularly when I was following all the rules. If life didn't make sense or felt particularly cruel, I was more likely to shake my fist and rail at the Creator of the universe than to let the doubt and the unanswered questions do their work.

Now I'm beginning to accept that doubt and uncertainty provide opportunities for my faith to go deeper. Some Christians see doubt and faith as strange bedfellows. But what if exploring the doubts and asking the hard questions are akin to repotting a root-bound plant that has outgrown its container?

Aging presents us with many opportunities to grow comfortable with paradox. To accept that though we're wise, there's much we don't know. To understand that the confidence we feel today might morph into uncertainty tomorrow. Doubts don't invalidate faith. In fact, if we can learn to live in "the promise of *and* in an *either-or* world," I believe that the roots of our faith will push through our doubt and go deep enough to hold fast, regardless of what the final chapter of life serves up.

RESTORATION: PIVOTING TOWARD HOPE AND WHOLENESS

Trauma and loss often take us into emotional spaces we'd much rather avoid. We might try to numb the pain by self-medicating with food, alcohol, or drugs, or by turning to counterfeit coping mechanisms such as shopping, extreme exercise, or zoning out in front of a screen. When the pain persists and hope begins to ebb, we might be tempted to check out and live as roommates in a peaceful yet chilly truce or cut our losses and reboot. If we want the pain to bear good fruit, we can't choose denial, escapism, or victimization. Instead, we have to ground ourselves in reality by confessing, forgiving, and facing our pain.

Confession. Confession might seem like a non sequitur in this chapter. After all, most of the traumas and losses we face are not attributable to our mistakes. What's the connection to confession? The truth is, we don't always respond brilliantly when we're in pain. Sometimes we react poorly or choose coping strategies that end up hurting us and those we love.

Furthermore, to be human is to sin. "If we claim we have no sin, we are only fooling ourselves and not living in the truth" (1 John 1:8).

While we often lack awareness about how our sinful tendencies affect those closest to us, marriage refuses to let us live in denial. Confession acknowledges what God—and our spouse—already know to be true.

Though we live in an age of oversharing, true biblical confession is an anomaly. If we want a marriage that's fulfilling, honest, and joyful, we all need to change, and confession is a sure catalyst. Based on our experiences, Christopher and I both believe that "no change takes place in marriage that does not begin with confession."

For the first forty years of my life, I habitually lied. I never defrauded the IRS or covered up an affair. My lies were small and seemingly insignificant. When Christopher asked if I was upset and I didn't want to be vulnerable, I passed off my edginess as fatigue. If lying about how much I spent on a new dress would prevent him from getting frustrated with me, I would lower the price by ten dollars without a second thought. I justified lying because I thought it was inconsequential. But the more I read the Bible, the more clear it became that God hates lying.

As the Holy Spirit convicted me, I tried to curb the behavior in isolation. It didn't take long for me to realize that I could not do this alone. I then confessed to Christopher and told him that my goal was to admit every time I lied about anything until I broke the habit. After about a year of faithfully confessing, I no longer found myself tempted to massage the truth.

Though confession should be a hallmark of a healthy relationship, few Christians regularly confess to their spouse or friends (James 5:16). Yes, it's mortifying. Yes, we will temporarily feel embarrassed and maybe even ashamed to admit that we watched porn, yelled at our child, or fantasized about retaliating for an offense. That mortification should cause us to think twice before we make the same mistake.

Inviting someone to hear our confession can be as simple as saying to your spouse or a friend, "I need to confess something. Can I ask you to hold this in confidence and speak forgiveness over me?"

And then be honest about what those sins are. No need to go into gory details, but you do need to be specific enough so that the listener knows what you're talking about (e.g., "I watched pornography for three hours this weekend" rather than "I spent too much time on the computer." Wink. Wink.). It's also beneficial to make an inventory of historic sins and confess them to our spouse. There's no good or biblical reason to keep secrets from each other. Additionally, honesty fosters both intimacy and trust.

Forgiveness and the role of empathy. For confession to become a normal part of our marriage, forgiveness must be practiced. If we fear that our confession will be used against us as an emotional battering ram, we'll find all kinds of excuses to keep quiet.

By the time we reach midlife, we have hurt others and been hurt thousands of times. Extending forgiveness should be routine. Unfortunately, that's not always the case. We can get stuck or even justify our decision to withhold forgiveness. However compelling our argument, we must remember that once we commit our lives to Christ, we give up our right to hold on to offenses or get even.

Though it might feel disingenuous to say "I forgive you" when we still feel angry or hurt, nowhere in Scripture does it say we have to *feel* like forgiving in order to release forgiveness. Forgiving is an act of obedience—not an emotion. I've repeatedly seen that when I align my actions with my core beliefs, my heart will follow. And when it doesn't, that typically indicates that I have more work to do.

Forgiveness does not deny wrongdoing. When our spouse confesses and we extend forgiveness, we're not minimizing the sin or saying "no big deal." We're acknowledging that something actually happened and simultaneously choosing not to leverage that sin to punish or shame them. Forgiveness is crucial for major sins (e.g., adultery, drug relapse, etc.) but equally imperative for minor offenses. In fact, if we don't regularly and thoroughly forgive the small things, they can eventually undermine our marriage.

There are at least two ways to tell if you're holding on to any residual unforgiveness. First, pay attention to your inner monologue. Is it characterized by love, affection, appreciation, and respect? Or are you grumbling against your spouse and ruminating on their perceived faults and mistakes? And second, are you open to being emotionally vulnerable and sexually intimate? Unforgiveness will muddy the waters of marriage, so keep forgiving until the waters run clear. I'm pretty sure that's what Jesus was referring to when he told Peter to forgive "seventy times seven" (Matthew 18:22).

While forgiveness is nonnegotiable and typically straightforward, restoration can be trickier. In certain situations we need to establish boundaries to protect ourselves and our children. If your spouse has recently confessed a major, long-term sin (e.g., an addiction or an affair), it would be wise to refrain from being intimate until they cut off the affair, gain a measure of sobriety, and are tested for STDs. Similarly, if your spouse has been physically or emotionally abusive, forgiving does not excuse their behavior. You may need to separate from them until your safety is guaranteed.

When we feel stuck or incapable of forgiving, empathy helps us to forgive. Empathy allows us to understand and feel from another's perspective. Feeling into, which is the German meaning for empathy, should enable us to refrain from judging and criticizing and instead extend compassion and grace. When the mob circled the woman caught in the act of adultery in John 8, Jesus' confrontative statement—"let the one who has never sinned throw the first stone!"—helps her accusers see their hypocrisy and to relate to her dilemma.

Empathy requires proximity, intentionality, and humility. Writer and pastor April Yamasaki elaborates, "Empathy begins with listening deeply to God and . . . other people. Rather than rushing in with well-meaning solutions of our own, we need to take the time to listen, to lament, and to live with the burden."

Jesus empathizes with our every need and every failure. By coming to earth as a vulnerable babe, born of blood and water, Jesus understands what it means to be human and live with needs and longings. He knows the pain of betrayal and the grief of losing a friend. Hebrews says, "We do not have a high priest who is unable to empathize with our weaknesses, but we have one who has been tempted in every way, just as we are—yet he did not sin" (Hebrews 4:15 NIV).

As Jesus demonstrated, empathy is a form of love. It should compel us to action. The apostle John wrote, "Dear children, let's not merely say that we love each other; let us show the truth by our actions" (1 John 3:18). This kind of incarnational love only happens as we fully forgive. This is the way of the cross—and the way to a fulfilling marriage.

Facing our pain. Regardless of what caused our pain, in order to get to the other side, we have to confront it head on. None of us ever want to do that. Author C. S. Lewis confirmed, "You would like to know how I behave when I am experiencing pain, not writing books about it. You need not guess, for I will tell you; I am a great coward. . . . If I knew any way of escape I would crawl through sewers to find it." My guess is most of us are like Lewis in this regard.

Even Jesus understood this temptation. As he knelt in the Garden of Gethsemane pleading with his Father to let the cup of suffering and death pass him by, Scripture tells us, "He prayed more fervently, and he was in such agony of spirit that his sweat fell to the ground like great drops of blood" (Luke 22:44).

Like Christ, most of us would prefer not to drink the cup filled with bitter dregs. But that's impossible. The oneness we have created actually increases our exposure to painful experiences. Sometimes, it can seem that the path to a fruitful, satisfying marriage goes directly through the Garden of Gethsemane. When our spouse loses their job, miscarries, or receives the worst-possible pathology

report, their pain is our pain. Denying or minimizing that reality
will only prolong it and increase our sense of loneliness. If we acknowledge what is evidently true, commit to accompanying one
another in our pain and grief, and invite in God's presence, his
kingdom will come. That's our only guarantee. And that's what got
Rick and Katherine through the season when they nearly lost
their son.

What did it look like for the two of you to go through the initial trauma
of watching your son almost die and then battle his addiction?

RICK   When faced with a crisis I tend to look to the future,
        thinking that if I plan well, everything will be re-
        solved, while Katherine tends to focus more on the
        past in hope of learning from what we did wrong.
        After our son's overdose we naturally defaulted to
        these tendencies. I relied on my relational and com-
        munication skills, believing that if my relationship
        with our son was good, everything would fall back
        into place. Katherine focused more on past mistakes
        and trying to make amends. Both of us, in our own
        ways, were wrongly assuming responsibility. It took
        some time before we could let go of trying to control
        things and be in the present, both before God and
        each other.

KATHERINE   Because of my tendency to focus on the past, I had
             many "if only" thoughts; if only we'd done this or
             that differently, our son would never have gone off
             the rails, which of course is tightly bound to regret.
             As with so many things on our journey, once I re-
             alized the destructive ways regret was affecting me, I

worked hard—and still am—to stay in the present. That practice was crucial because there was never one single moment when everything changed for the better; our son's healing came incrementally. Things improved little by little.

How did your faith affect this journey?

KATHERINE   When one of us was disabled by sorrow or fear or doubt or confusion, the other would carry that pain. When Rick was weak, I was strong, and (far more often) when I was weak, Rick was strong. In fact, at one point when I felt like my very faith might not survive, he came to me and said, "I'll believe for you." And it's true, he did believe for me when my faith was breaking apart. Another time we were sitting outside the hospital and he broke down. I hugged him and prayed for him. He couldn't handle another thing right then, so I just kind of let him know it was okay not to handle it. The grace that I had for him and he had for me made it easier to support each other and confess our failures to one another.

RICK   Because of other difficulties in our life, we were already in the habit of trusting God for many things.

KATHERINE   I've thought much about how hard it would have been if we didn't begin earnestly praying together, literally begging God to save our son. I know this had everything to do with both our son's recovery and our marriage growing stronger during that time. We needed God and we needed each other, and if any one of us was missing in our like-minded triptych, I doubt we'd be where we are now.

What's life like for you today?

RICK   We feel relief because of how many years have passed since his overdose, but things will never be exactly the same. Christ needs to be our son's foundation and his first love. Katherine and I need to learn how to totally trust God for our son's well-being rather than constantly monitoring how he's doing.

KATHERINE   He just got married, which on one level comes with that "happily ever after" vibe so prevalent in our culture. And it is a precious thing and a gift from God. But still, there is no sparkly bow signifying the end of all bad things in his life. My peace comes from knowing that no matter what, God will continue to draw our son to himself. We pray for him every day. Though the trauma is now past tense, our lives will never return to what they were before that fateful night.

$\sim\!\!\!\sim$

As Rick and Katherine experienced, trauma and loss change us and our marriages. When we cleave to each other and allow Christ to comfort and transform us, he will prove that he is the God of redemption. He will use every tear and every heartbreak to help us become more like him, and to love our spouse with an ever-deepening resolve.

GOING DEEPER

1. What losses and traumas are you facing or have you faced in midlife? What about prior to midlife? How have they affected your marriage? Have you gotten the help you need to process any traumatic events?

2. How have trauma and loss affected your faith?

3. What's your default when you are in pain? What's your spouse's? Is there room for growth? If so, what would that look like?

4. If confession is not a regular part of your life, what would it take to integrate it into your life? What's the cost if you don't confess?

5. What's your empathy quotient? Which comes more naturally for you: empathizing and moving closer or judging and moving away? How does this pattern affect your marriage?

CHAPTER SEVEN

CREATED TO CONNECT

How Attachment Issues Affect Marriage

D oug and Renée are an energetic, highly accomplished couple who both work as writers. Though they have a strong marriage and share common goals, they differ in many ways. According to Doug,

> I'm a morning person. Renée is a night owl. I'm a planner. She helps me to have fun. She's a hugger and very empathetic. It's hard to go out to eat with her because everyone wants to talk to her. People are scared to approach me.

As is the case for many couples, these differences sometimes make it difficult for them to connect, particularly when they're in conflict. Renée fleshes this out:

> If Doug and I are on the same page about finances, child rearing, or work, then the lack of conflict makes it easy for us to connect emotionally. If any of those things are awry, then we turn from each other. I feel like my attachment efforts are rejected because he's focused on resolving something that, in his mind, is more important.

In his defense, Doug explains,

My MO is typically, "I got stuff I gotta do." I'm going to make sure I keep up with things so that while we're trying to figure out what's happening, I don't put myself in a bigger hole. I keep going.

Renée and Doug always find their way back to each other, but both can feel frustrated when there's distance between them.

Occasionally feeling disconnected from our spouse is completely normal. If the disconnect happens frequently or results in intense conflict, it can become problematic. Thankfully, it's never too late to learn how to connect. By identifying and addressing the specific causality of our disconnect and then vulnerably moving toward each other, we can develop the kind of oneness God intended.

ATTACHMENT 101

"*Bonding* is the ability to establish an emotional attachment to another person. It's the ability to relate to another on the deepest level." British psychologist John Bowlby pioneered bonding and attachment research in the mid-1900s. His detractors criticized his theories as one-dimensional and deterministic, but today many psychologists and therapists believe the principles of attachment theory not only help parents meet their children's developmental needs but can also help adult couples connect more deeply and more consistently.

There are valid reasons why some of us might resist exploring attachment issues. The premise can feel either too abstract or, as Bowlby's naysayers believed, overly reductionistic. We might feel hopeless that something so deeply embedded could ever change, or we might be inclined to dismiss the possibility that our early relational deficits could continue to affect us because they happened so long ago. Some may prefer to trust the false adage that time heals all wounds rather than exhume painful memories.

Attachment issues are worth exploring for at least two reasons. First, the underlying premise of attachment theory as applied to marital therapy is that intimate, committed relationships are capable of healing deep wounds like nothing else. And second, human development happens in stages that build on each other. When we move forward chronologically without having a sense of who we are and how we relate to those around us, the rest of our lives can be out of plumb. According to Bowlby's findings, "Without a secure base established in infancy, humans from childhood throughout adult life may develop and cling to the belief that the world is unstable and that they cannot safely trust others." This is the opposite of God's design.

We cannot survive without others. Though we are the most intelligent species on earth, we are also the most dependent on parental care for the longest period of time. By intentionally designing human development in this fashion, God gives us the opportunity to learn how to bond with others so we can gradually move toward having reciprocal relationships.

Not only did God set up the universe to facilitate connection, the Trinity models and embodies intimate connectedness. The Father, Son, and Holy Spirit exist and interact as a community who always have and always will love each other. This foundational characteristic informs who we are. In *Changes That Heal*, therapist Henry Cloud states,

> Relationship, or bonding, is at the foundation of God's nature. Since we are created in his likeness, relationship is our most fundamental need, the very foundation of who we are. Without relationship, without attachment to God and others, we can't be our true selves. We can't be truly human.

The first book of the Bible confirms the importance of relationship: "The LORD God said, 'It is not good for the man to be alone. I will make a helper suitable for him'" (Genesis 2:18 NIV). Aloneness was the only aspect of God's creation that was deemed lacking. God remedies this by creating an *ezer kenegdo,* or warrior ally, for Adam. Adam immediately recognizes the wonder of this co-laborer. In one of the most beautiful pieces of poetry ever written, he declares,

"At last! . . .

This one is bone from my bone,
and flesh from my flesh!
She will be called 'woman,'
because she was taken from 'man.'"

This explains why a man leaves his father and mother and is joined to his wife, and the two are united into one. (Genesis 2:23-24)

Uniting or cleaving is akin to bonding, which is God's desire for us as married couples. To achieve this, some of us will need to explore how our early childhood relationships might complicate or prevent us from bonding with our spouse.

As infants and children, when we express our needs and our parents or caregivers become attuned to those needs and then lovingly, consistently meet them, we internalize four essential truths: needs are good (i.e., being needy is normal and acceptable), expressing needs results in connection, others can be trusted to meet our needs, and we are worthy of love. These lessons become the foundation on which all future relationships are built—including our marriage and our relationship with God.

Practically speaking, this means when a baby wakes up crying, the mother understands that her child is trying to communicate "I'm scared" or "I'm cold." Instinctively, she then tenderly scoops up the baby, makes eye contact, offers comforting coos, holds and settles the child. By doing this again and again (and again!), the mother becomes a kind of emotional umbilical cord, wooing the child into life.

The ongoing responses between a mother and child allow the baby to develop a sense of self and a sense of well-being. Once this is established, children then begin to believe they can depend on others to meet their needs and that the world is a safe, predictable place. This process of bonding with mother (and father or other caregivers) typically takes two years. It is only after a child has bonded that they can begin to individuate or learn that they are a separate entity from mother. When all goes well, by the time children are two or three, they have internalized their parents' acceptance and approval and are able to attach to others. If this kind of consistent, loving care happened rarely, we might still be trying to get our basic attachment needs met.

Though not all marital problems point back to an inability to bond, it's likely that this deficit factors into our overall marital contentment more than we imagine. Attachment issues might be the culprit if we routinely experience unproductive conflict, regularly feel disconnected or insecure, struggle to trust each other, or overreact to criticism.

Attachment issues can surface at any time, but seasons of stress, trauma, and loss tend to widen any pre-existing relational gaps. Because the "longer partners feel disconnected, the more negative their interactions become," by midlife, some couples may conclude that they will never consistently connect. However real that feeling is, research confirms that we can overcome our deficits and learn how to connect at any age. The first step is understanding our unique attachment style.

ATTACHMENT STYLES

In *Becoming Attached*, psychologist Robert Karen explains that early in life "one forms images of the self and others and of how they fit together, which have a powerful hold on the personality and serve as a blueprint for future relationships." These blueprints lead to either a secure or an insecure attachment style.

Securely attached adults believe they are lovable, are aware of their limitations, and are comfortable asking for help. When a couple is securely attached, they are more resilient in the face of significant challenges, can have productive conflicts, and are able to offer each other empathy—all of which build trust. Feeling safe and known then fosters emotional and physical intimacy.

By contrast, we tend toward one of the three insecure attachment styles if we failed to bond well or experienced trauma. There are many possible explanations for failure to bond, but often it's because our parents or caregivers were either emotionally disconnected from us or unavailable, perhaps due to chronic sickness, divorce, or mental health issues. Insecure attachment can also result if we were consistently shamed or ignored when we expressed needs as infants and young children. Insecure attachment becomes like a flawed blueprint that makes it more difficult to connect with and trust our spouse. Please remember that the goal of exploring potential attachment issues is not to blame our parents for any current relational struggles, but rather to help us understand why we might be missing each other.

Insecure attachment manifests as anxious, avoidant, or disorganized relationship style. Adults who have an anxious attachment style worry about minor fluctuations in their partner's moods (which sometimes leads to jealousy) and anticipate or even expect rejection or abandonment, particularly during conflict. When fears or insecurities surface, anxiously attached adults may try to control or manipulate their partner in the hope of gaining reassurance. This can be Renée's default when she and Doug are in conflict.

Avoidantly attached adults tend to prefer autonomy to intimate, interdependent relationships. They see commitment as constrictive and may come off as aloof. Additionally, adults with an avoidant attachment style have a highly sensitive radar for manipulation that, when triggered, compels them to disengage in an effort to maintain control and autonomy. When in conflict, Doug tends toward an avoidant style of attachment.

Finally, disorganized attachment occurs when parents are unable to discern and provide for their children's emotional and physical needs or when the child has experienced trauma, abuse, or neglect. Adults who grew up in such environments may trust others too quickly, making them vulnerable to abusive relationships. They also find it easier to focus on others' needs while detaching from their own.

Identifying our unique attachment style is one component of bonding with, or attaching to, our spouse.

THE WHY OF OUR DISCONNECT

There are at least five potential reasons why married couples fail to consistently connect: mismatched attachment styles, childhood trauma or neglect, personality differences, issues connected to being on the autism spectrum, and remarriage.

Mismatched attachment styles. Though Christopher and I knew nothing about attachment theory during round one of our relationship (which ended in a broken engagement), we now know that mismatched attachment styles contributed to our demise. It took two years of counseling, prayer, and self-reflection before we finally understood this.

As a teenager, I carried a great deal of anxiety and insecurity, particularly when conflict surfaced in dating relationships. Because disagreements often resulted in breakups, I came to believe that any conflict—no matter how insignificant—would end in abandonment. Abandonment is one of "the primary fears of all human beings." To avoid being abandoned, I subtly manipulated people when I sensed they were angry with me. That dynamic was one of the main reasons that Christopher broke off our first engagement—which of course reinforced my worst fears.

My fear-based responses triggered Christopher, in part because his mom was also dishonest about her emotional needs. He recounts,

> My mother and I could connect emotionally, but she would use this connection to address her own needs that were unmet by my father. This blurred the boundaries between us and caused me to feel consistently manipulated. As I sought autonomy, she became jealous and clingy. Essentially, I learned love from a mother who often made the relationship about her. I now suspect that she had undiagnosed clinical depression for much of her adult life, which helps me to be more sympathetic with her. Defensiveness and narcissism, which I'm still trying to root out, became coping mechanisms and ways of individuating.

Narcissistic tendencies are fairly common for avoidantly attached men. Narcissists are inordinately focused on *their* needs, *their* experiences, and *their* feelings. Early on, Christopher and I were a perfectly imperfect pair: I denied my needs and instead focused on his, which reinforced and further inflated his narcissistic tendencies.

Attachment alarms go off when we feel ashamed or vulnerable, or "when we perceive a negative shift in our sense of connection to a loved one." During conflict, insecurely attached couples tend to get stuck in unproductive loops marked by blame, withdrawal, manipulation, defensiveness, or worst-case-scenario thinking. The maddening push and pull can make it feel impossible to connect.

Trauma and neglect. Our ability to have meaningful, intimate relationships may also be compromised if neglect or trauma happened during our formative years. The authors of *Bonding* believe that "security, or the lack of it, has reverberations far into our later lives."

Neglect happens when our spiritual, physical, and emotional needs are not consistently met. Few parents intentionally neglect their children. Nevertheless, parents with long-term health issues (including addictive behaviors) are often incapable of providing for their children's needs. Military deployments or working multiple jobs can also result in neglect. Neglect can cause children to feel unworthy, unwanted, ashamed, angry, and ambivalent about their needs. When a child is neglected, they are left to fend for themselves, which may result in an insecure attachment style and fierce independence.

Like neglect, experiencing trauma leads to difficulty connecting and even a kind of disintegration of the soul. Because trauma changes how the brain processes information, it can leave us either expecting the worst, or cut off and compartmentalized—both of which impede our ability to connect with our spouse. Dr. Bessel van der Kolk's research revealed that all trauma affects intimate relationships: "After you have experienced something so unspeakable, how do you learn to trust yourself or anyone else again?" Learning how and who to trust is essential if we hope to become securely attached.

Personality differences. Even though God intentionally designed each of us to be unique, our innate differences can result in disconnection. Every human being has a distinct way of perceiving and moving through the world. This is awesome—except when it's not.

Christopher and I are incredibly different people. When we took the Myers-Briggs Type Indicator in premarital counseling, we were off the charts—in opposite directions. He's an extreme extrovert, and I'm an extreme introvert. He's a feeler and a perceiver. I'm a thinker and a judger. His ability to compartmentalize is both enviable and maddening. He considers a vacation successful only when we're active every moment of every day. I love exploring and hiking, but I also love sitting down to eat. While it's true that these differences make our marriage rich and spicy, they sometimes cause indigestion.

After nearly thirty years together, it would seem that we *should have* figured out how to overlook or even embrace our many differences. And sometimes we can. Praise God for those days! But there are moments when the smallest and most incidental of behaviors (like your spouse's habit of sneezing dramatically or chewing with their mouth open) can trigger a visceral, negative reaction. Perhaps few couples are as fundamentally different as we are, but "all relationships require translation." Tools such as the Myers-Briggs or Enneagram can aid us in the translation process. If used properly, they should help us to better understand each other and motivate us toward compassion rather than judgment.

Conversely, personality assessments can also lead us to dismissively put others in boxes and generate excuses for our own bad behavior (e.g., "Yes, I'm frequently angry, but I'm an Enneagram One. What do you expect?"). Any insight gleaned from these tools will strengthen our marriages only if we commit to honor and respect each other. If we perceive our spouse as less than because their differentness inconveniences or annoys us, we've missed God's intention in creating us as sacred others.

While it's advantageous for us to conclude that the irritations indicate our spouse needs to change, if we allow them to become an impetus for us to change, then we can move closer to each other. Christopher and I have been proactively and intentionally changing for the whole of our marriage. He doesn't get angry as often, and I'm now willing to admit that anger is a thing for me. He has learned to value being backstage, and I'm learning to be comfortable on center stage. We've discovered that kayaking satisfies his desire to verbally process and my need to engage physically. He sits in the rear, talking and paddling. I sit in the front and listen as I enjoy the view. We are growing.

Autism spectrum issues. When one spouse is on the autism spectrum, a marriage may face unique attachment challenges. Mental health practitioners first listed infantile autism in the *DSM-III* in 1980. Seven years later, a more nuanced explanation of autism was added. In 1994 *DSM-IV* included Asperger's syndrome, which is now within the diagnosis of autism spectrum disorder (ASD). This timeline is important because many individuals born prior to the mid-1990s who have milder forms of ASD, such as Asperger's syndrome, were probably never diagnosed.

Spectrum disorders manifest in a wide array of behaviors. One common characteristic is that those on the autism spectrum are easily overstimulated by what most adults would consider normal human interactions, such as making eye contact, giving or receiving physical affection, and reading other's emotions. My friend Rachel describes what it has been like to be married to her husband, who has ASD.

> One of the hardest things has been reconciling my husband's immense intelligence (he is in a niche job where his intellect is prized) with his inability to complete seemingly simple, everyday tasks. He frequently forgets to wear deodorant or take his daily medication and often loses things. He is an introvert and will rarely initiate conversation about daily life or sense my need for it. He can spend hours deep in thought on a coding problem or immersed in a book and dislikes it when I interrupt to ask him a mundane question.
>
> His struggle to interpret body language or subtle social cues means that I have to be very direct about what I need. He often won't notice or respond to my subtle indicators of displeasure, like sighing heavily or crashing around the kitchen as I empty the dishwasher. Instead, I've learned that I need to be specific and direct: "After dinner, can I have thirty minutes to talk to you uninterrupted?" I occasionally long to have a partner who would intuitively sense what I need. But in so many other ways he is an amazing husband and father. He's kind, generous, and sacrificial. Learning to be more upfront about my needs seems like a worthwhile trade-off.

Spouses not on the autism spectrum may wonder how someone who is so proficient, even genius in some areas, can be so remedial in others. Because individuals with ASD tend to have exemplary gifting, it can be easy to assume that they're not even trying in the relational realm. More often than not, they're simply playing to their strengths—which we all do.

Though challenging, attachment is definitely possible if one spouse is on the autism spectrum. But because relationships are built on core behaviors such as good communication, empathy, and affection, learning how to connect when you're married to someone on the autism spectrum takes a tremendous amount of intentionality and grace. According to Rachel, "It helps to remember that we're a team and that each member brings different skills to the table to benefit the whole. Our skillsets are complementary, not congruent."

Remarriage. According to a 2014 study done by the Pew Research Center, 67 percent of adults between the ages of fifty-five and sixty-four who have been widowed or divorced will remarry. For those who remarry after a divorce, learning how to attach might be complicated if abuse, abandonment, or infidelity took place in a previous marriage. Even if the divorce was amicable and one has done the hard work of forgiving and processing what went wrong, there may be certain situations that activate out-of-proportion reactions.

Because divorce is traumatic, ongoing communication about any feelings of abandonment, fear, or hurt will be key in moving toward a secure attachment. Remarriage after divorce requires that any alliances or emotional ties with the first spouse be severed and new boundaries set so that one can fully bond with a new spouse. Thankfully, no one has to stop loving a former spouse in order to love well in a subsequent marriage. God created our hearts to have an unlimited capacity to love.

For widows and widowers, one of the main challenges is discerning how to honor the past without being bound by it. Several friends who remarried after their spouses died said they wanted to celebrate wedding anniversaries or mark their deceased spouses' birthdays but felt uncertain about how to do that sensitively. They also expressed the insecurity they sometimes feel when waves of grief wash over them and they have to decide if or how to share these feelings with their new spouse.

Lessons learned in the first marriage can help couples to do things differently the second time around. According to my friend Diana,

> The trauma of losing our first marriages (mine ending by death and his by a divorce he did not want) resulted in both of us valuing the fight required to make this marriage work. The hills we once died on in our former marriages seem so much less important. The massive, deep chasm of loss that we both stared into forced us to consider anew the sacredness of marriage. This is a good thing, but it can sometimes be problematic. Such as when we feel like we can't or shouldn't bring up what feels like pedestrian concerns (yard work, dishes, etc.), which is the stuff of life. Ten years in and holding out for a low-conflict ideal based on valuing what's most important can at times feel like a limiting constraint.

Negotiations and recalibrations of this type can take on a heightened sense of importance for couples who remarry. The desire to get it right raises the stakes and the tension. But couples who remarry often feel profoundly grateful for a second chance. That gratitude enables them to extend an abundance of grace and mercy to each other.

Any of these five issues can make connecting difficult, but none of them are a death knell for marriage. God created us to grow, and the Holy Spirit empowers transformation. Once we identify what's going on, we can interrupt unhealthy cycles and shift the relational dynamic toward greater health.

LEARNING TO CONNECT

Moving toward a more secure attachment takes time and demands deliberateness. The first step is recognizing when we feel disconnected and then working backward to discern what preceded or provoked that feeling. Was it conflict? A harshly spoken word? Our spouse's weekend habit of binge-watching Netflix that leaves us feeling abandoned?

One of the many gifts of midlife is that we begin to have enough self-knowledge and humility to pause and discern the essence of our issues. When we can admit that something is amiss, identify what that something is, and then talk about it from the perspective of our needs (versus what we perceive our spouse might have done wrong), we can begin to move toward each other.

For example, I recently felt anxiety about my increasing pain levels and what that might mean in terms of my ability to be a warrior ally in our marriage. In the past I would have withdrawn or been annoyed that Christopher did not intuit my dilemma. This time I directly communicated my insecurity about how he might react if my health continued to decline and asked for reassurance. He acknowledged my concern, expressed sorrow about the seemingly intractable nature of my illness, and then affirmed that he's not going anywhere. Circumstantially, nothing changed, but the emotional connection that we made mitigated my fears.

These conversations require self-awareness and vulnerability. Like my friend Rachel, we tend to prefer—and sometimes expect—a spouse who instinctively knows what we need so that we don't have to ask for it. Prophetic, servant-minded spouses would certainly make life easier. To some extent this reflects a desire for our spouse to be more like us, which is understandable but apparently not what God had in mind. Our differentness calls us into the deep waters of vulnerability. If Christopher intuitively understood that I wanted more tenderness without me saying a word, I wouldn't have to risk anything. It's in the risking, the putting it out there, that we learn how to trust each other more fully.

Many of us are well aware that expressing our needs does not necessarily mean that our spouse will immediately—or maybe ever—be able to meet those needs. It often takes years to change ingrained relational patterns. As we wait for our spouse to come through, we have to remain in an unguarded posture. If we resort to insecure or manipulative behaviors (like blaming or withdrawing), we may stall any progress.

Do talk about what it's like to wait, but do so from a place of need. I'm embarrassed to admit that I find it much easier to criticize Christopher than to express my needs. My default tends to be "Why are you withholding words from me? Why can't you just tell me what you know I want to hear?" rather than "I'm really struggling to wait well for you. I feel powerless and exposed, which I don't like." The latter expression is soft and vulnerable while the former is harsh and accusatory. If you're the one being asked to change, it's helpful to communicate that you haven't forgotten your spouse's request even if you're not currently able to meet their need.

Our spouse's inability or unwillingness to provide for our needs can result in disconnection and pain, particularly if we have been clear and they have neither met us nor made much of an effort to meet us (at least from our perspective). If our spouse resists growing or demonstrates a hard heart, we may be at a loss to know how to stay vulnerable and continue loving. In such situations the following responses might help.

First, reach out to friends to meet the needs that are not specific to marriage. My desire to pray with others exceeds Christopher's desire. In the past I tried to convince him to pray more frequently and then judged him when he declined. No surprise, this went poorly. It works better for us when I regularly get together with female friends to pray. We do have to be careful not to form emotionally dependent relationships that might jeopardize our marriage. That's what happened for Scot and Camille.

Second, as detailed in chapter five, evaluate whether or not the expectations you hold are realistic based on who you married. Many of us come into marriage believing that our spouse should be our soulmate who meets our every need. That would be awesome, but no human can do that. During the past twenty-nine years, Christopher and I have realized that there are certain completely reasonable expectations that we may never be able to satisfy. Make no mistake: *this is really hard.* But when we grieve it as a loss and choose to love anyway, we will find our way through.

Trying to meet our spouse's needs is fundamental to the overall health of our marriage. This can be particularly complicated in midlife because needs are not static: they change based on many factors. The ways we connected as a couple in our twenties and thirties may not work in our forties, fifties, or sixties. Additionally, though you and your spouse might have similar big-picture needs, the specifics often vary. Unless they completely overlap, we may have to willingly set our needs aside so that we can meet our spouse's needs. When both parties commit to this type of sacrificial lifestyle, our needs get met and our attachment deepens.

Finally, if the need is realistic and can't be met by anyone other than your spouse (like sexual intimacy), don't give up. As much as you are able, keep praying, keep needing, keep loving. And find a good counselor who will support your worldview. The waiting can be excruciating, but it keeps us in a posture of dependence on God. That's a good thing.

Though many of us received a faulty attachment blueprint and may struggle to consistently connect with our spouse, there's no reason to lose hope. If either spouse grows more secure, the relationship will benefit. This happens, at least in part, as we experience more of God's love and receive healing for our relational deficits. Renée and Doug are working toward this goal.

Can you describe your behavior when you're not connecting emotionally?

RENÉE   I go to my room, or if that's not an option, I'll put on my headphones and listen to some sad music and cry or sing. I may take a bath. Sometimes it takes me a few minutes to move through my frustration and sometimes it takes days.

DOUG   I'm usually trying to find an opportunity to process what the problem is. Maybe six or eight times out of ten I don't even know what I did to make her upset. When I ask, she's so angry that I'm not even sure what the issue is. So I'm going to do something to deal with it. Maybe I'll exercise or go running. And I'm going to go to resources, whether it be a book or Scripture or talking to a friend or an accountability partner.

What's going on emotionally when you can't connect?

RENÉE   I'm ashamed of feeling needy, and then I get angry. Sometimes there's deep sadness and regret. I wonder, *Where did we go wrong? Maybe I shouldn't have put my career first. Maybe I should have been a homemaker.* I definitely don't feel heard during these times, and that exacerbates things and makes me want to withdraw even more. One of the challenges is that Doug may not share my concern. I'm up here [gestures with her hands above her head], and he's like, "We're fine," which makes me even angrier.

DOUG   I can feel a lot of anger, contempt, and verbal shots coming from Renée. Having the person you love say unkind things is not easy to receive, and it's more painful when my kids hear them. Sometimes I'm in a better place to respond, but they take their toll. I feel disrespected at these times, and as a guy, that makes me feel unable to connect. I need time to calm down.

RENÉE   The way I describe our dynamic is that I am the waves crashing into the shoreline. Doug is the deep, still water. He says he's stable and calm, but I do feel a sense of churning.

It's hard to discern what's going on with Doug. I can't always tell, and I've known him for over twenty years. Sometimes I feel he's not only being stable but that he's wearing a mask and protecting his innermost emotions from the outside world. I want to be let in.

DOUG   Most times I'm thinking about and processing a lot of stuff. It might just be my thinking and processing look. Am I actually defending or protecting myself? I don't know. I had a mother who was very critical, and I'm sure I developed a certain demeanor to protect myself from her scrutiny. Part of it is being one of a few African Americans in a predominantly white town. I played sports through college, and when you're in an athletic competition, you don't want your opponent to know you're exhausted, so you learn how to keep a game face on. I'm sure all those things are happening.

What has it been like to work on or change this dynamic?

DOUG   I have a coach I work with, and every time something comes up that we need to work on I'll go with Renée to her therapist. We have checkups just like with the car.

RENÉE   We also pray together. We go to the marriage retreats at our church every year.

DOUG   It's important to remember that the speed of change or progress in marriage depends on lots of things, such as our health, outside stressors (such as having teenagers), and careers. Some of those stressors can be a great impetus to grow. Challenges can instigate change, but when you have stressors, it slows things down. Change in a marriage is dialectic. You change as it relates to your maturity and to your spouse's maturity.

When do you feel most connected? What's the glue that holds you together even though you have different temperaments and attachment styles?

DOUG   Decision-making. What do we want our future to be regarding our family, vacations, career, parenting?

RENÉE   Sex. Going for a walk, bike riding, traveling. When the kids go away to a camp, it's a honeymoon for us. There's less stress. He's my boyfriend again.

DOUG   Our faith keeps us together even though we practice it differently. Our devotions are as different as we are, but we go to Sunday worship together. We make a family budget. We parent together. We have a commitment to a weekly date and a commitment to pray. You've got to have those things in place if you want to stay united.

RENÉE   If anyone in the world gets me, it's Doug. People may misunderstand me, but I want to be able to go home and feel like I have a sanctuary and that my husband really gets me. If anyone is going to be honest with me about needing to change course, it's going to be my husband.

Our deepest longing is to connect with God and each other. As we come to understand the attachment styles present in our marriage and work to meet each other's needs, we can fulfill God's call to love each other—and in the process, truly become one.

GOING DEEPER

1. How do you and your spouse's attachment styles differ? How do they overlap? How do these similarities and differences help or hinder you from connecting?

2. How did you relate to your parents and siblings when you were growing up? (Specifically, was there a lot of unconditional love, affection, and affirmation or not so much?) If you did not grow up receiving unconditional love and acceptance, how has this affected your marriage?

3. What are the main personality differences between you and your spouse and how have they affected your marriage (positively and negatively)?

4. What specific kind of support, connection, and affection do you need from your spouse to feel known and accepted? What does it look like to talk openly about these needs?

5. When you feel disconnected from your spouse, how do you react/ respond? Do you ever try to control or manipulate them? Are you more likely to withdraw? Please explore both the long- and short-term effects these choices might have on your partner.

CHAPTER EIGHT

SEX, PART 1

How Did We Get Here?

M ichael was thirteen when he heard his first teaching on extreme abstinence. For the next eight years he struggled to integrate his faith with an ideology that categorized sexual desire and any sexual expression outside of marriage as sinful. This philosophy left him feeling disconnected from his body and ashamed when he felt aroused or experienced sexual desire. He explains,

> My body was diminished by this teaching in terms of its relevance to my life in general and my spiritual life specifically. Sex was discussed only in terms of warnings. For example, kissing will lead to intercourse and therefore was forbidden. The teachings never helped me understand how to have healthy nonsexual touch and definitely discouraged any kind of sexual touch. I turned off my sexuality, or rather the switch never got turned on. I didn't really understand myself as a sexual being. From that place, very little self-knowledge was possible.

We live in a world where it's unimaginable to go through a single day without being barraged by hypersexualized imagery. And yet it's incredibly countercultural to talk about our bodies and our sexuality in an honest, respectful fashion—even as adults.

This is not a new problem. Nor is it only a church problem. Both religious and secular culture have largely failed to offer a healthy, balanced perspective of sexuality. Many of us who are currently in midlife were most likely inculcated by one of two diametrically opposed philosophies regarding sex: the anything goes, no-rules-apply approach (prevalent in the 1960s and 1970s) or the highly repressive everything-is-forbidden approach of the extreme abstinence movement. Neither of these ideologies accurately captures God's intent. Furthermore, both tend to leave lasting wounds that need to be addressed.

This first of two chapters on sex will refute the extremes and explore barriers to healthy intimacy. The latter includes faulty teaching, sins (those we've committed and those others have committed against us), cultural conditioning, and shame. As we remove the obstacles and make sense of our backstory, God's good news will apply to the marriage bed.

MISSING THE MARK

Scripture provides clear parameters and guidelines for sex and sexuality, starting in the early chapters of the first book. As stated in Genesis and then reiterated by Jesus, "A man leaves his father and mother and is *joined* to his wife, and the two are *united into one* (Matthew 19:5, emphasis added). Sexual relationships outside of marriage are forbidden (see Exodus 20:14; Hebrews 13:4) and though some of the male heroes in the Old Testament deviated from this, God's plan is—and always has been—monogamy. The Bible promotes mutuality in the bedroom (1 Corinthians 7), and offers us three overarching purposes for marital sex: procreation, bonding, and pleasure.

Despite this clarity, confusion and misinformation often prevail. This is partially attributable to the enemy's strategic attack against God's creation. Satan understands that by design, sex within a covenanted marriage relationship is intended to be transcendent and revelatory; good marital sex points us to God. As Jay Stringer writes in *Unwanted*, "Evil hates the beauty of sex, and because it cannot abolish its existence, it works to corrupt its essence." Sex trafficking, hookup culture, sexual abuse, using sex as a means of control, and the production and consumption of pornography are all forms of corruption.

The narrative of broken sexuality is so powerful and so pervasive that it can make us forget that our faith should help us to understand, integrate, and steward our sexuality. We serve a God who asks us to surrender the whole of who we are to him—including our genitalia. If that seems hyperbolic, remember that God required circumcision as a sign of his covenant, effectively saying, "Even this—male genitalia—needs to be submitted to me." How many of us have ever heard that preached on a Sunday morning?

The church's failure to clarify and uphold God's creative intentions for human sexuality has resulted in tremendous personal pain and to some extent a loss of credibility. This happens whenever the church abdicates responsibility, follows cultural norms, overlooks sexual indiscretions—particularly by its leaders—or swings wildly in the opposite direction and becomes controlling. These two polar opposites manifest as anything goes or extreme abstinence. The former aims to remove all barriers, including godly shame. The latter uses shame to hem us in. Both miss the mark.

Sex without borders. The anything-goes version of sexuality (currently rebranded as the sex positive movement) purports that sexual desires are of ultimate importance and, provided that no one is physically harmed, should be pursued without reservation. Though this is perhaps best epitomized by the free love generation of the 1960s, such beliefs and behaviors have always existed (see Romans 1).

As part of the larger cultural pushback against authority, moral restraint was neither highly valued nor widely practiced during the sixties and seventies. If you are between the ages of fifty and seventy and did not grow up in a conservative Christian home, the anything-goes mindset probably influenced your adolescence and early adulthood. When I was in high school during the mid- to late 1970s, heavy drinking, pot smoking, and sexual exploration were normal weekend activities. Such formative experiences can leave us with powerful memories (some good, some bad), shame, and the tendency to look longingly over our shoulder at what was. One male friend has never been content with his intimate life as a married man, largely because he continues to compare his middle-aged wife to his college lovers.

No sex and lots of borders. The extreme abstinence movement represents the opposite perspective. Michael and thousands of other men and women have been taught that you become damaged goods if you engage in any kind of sexual behavior prior to marriage. Youth leaders used scare tactics to drive this point home. In one iteration, a cup was passed around the circle and each teen was instructed to spit in it. When it arrived back at the starting point, the leader communicated that premarital sex rendered everyone equivalent to the contents of the now-vile cup: disgusting and undesirable. Teachings of this ilk rely on shame and fear to expunge sexual desire and corral sexual expression.

This philosophy can be traced back to ancient Gnostic teachings that erroneously divided the world into two separate realms: the spiritual and the material. Gnostics (from the Greek word *gnosis* or *knowledge*) denied Jesus' incarnation and his bodily resurrection. Because they believed the corporeal world, including our bodies and sex, to be inherently evil, their understanding of sexuality and bodily pleasure became terribly warped. The Gnostics' misguided mindset has endured through the centuries and continues to seep into the church's teaching on sexuality. In *Faithful: A Theology of Sex*, Beth Felker Jones states, "Christians, like the Gnostics, have sometimes had a hard time imagining what it could mean to be both sexual and redeemed."

To some extent, the church has always struggled to integrate healthy sexuality with healthy spirituality. That struggle was manifested in the purity culture movement that started during the 1980s. Purity culture teachings provided a strong pushback to the licentiousness of the '60s and '70s, and aimed to prevent teens from contracting sexually transmitted diseases and the HIV virus. Joshua Harris's book *I Kissed Dating Goodbye* (1997) capitalized on this wave, but earlier books also promoted extreme abstinence (e.g., Elizabeth Elliot's 1984 classic *Passion and Purity*). I'm using the purity culture as an example not because it was the first or only version of extreme abstinence teaching, but because it's the most recent example and it affected many evangelical Christians who are now in midlife.

The purity culture movement determined that the best way to avoid sexual immorality (as defined by the movement) was to erect fences around fences. Leaders determined that dating was ungodly and that any form of arousal or physical engagement (including kissing) was sinful—until marriage. Once married an internal switch would be magically flipped, facilitating awesome, orgasmic sex from day one. Scripture clearly communicates that God calls us to celibacy until marriage, but when manipulation, fear, and shame are employed to enforce that call, the damaging effects often linger even after the switch gets flipped.

Sophie, now in her early forties, and her husband were among those for whom the purity culture teaching was detrimental. She shared the following:

I was terrified of sex. Our whole wedding night was carefully choreographed to mitigate pain. Instead of busting through the hotel room door and having a hot and heavy make-out session that naturally led to intercourse, we tiptoed through the whole night. We didn't end up having intercourse for days. And I didn't actually enjoy sex for over a year. I now believe that it wasn't just fear of literal pain but the natural result of years and years of teachings that equated sex, sexuality, and sexual feelings with sin and shame.

Purity culture teaching on sexuality is very formulaic. A (if you stay "pure" until marriage) + B (you marry a strong Christian man/woman) = C (you will be blessed with a wonderful, immediately sexually fulfilling, godly marriage). I ticked each of those boxes, but right off the bat we were not living the C part of that equation. And it terrified me. When you are taught such rigid formulas, there is no room for nuance, for personalities, and for challenges that might come your way.

It has taken years to get a realistic perspective of my own body, a man's body, and what fulfills me sexually.

Sophie's experience is not unusual. Many people, both inside and outside of the church, reduce Christian morality to an expansive list of rules. In its purest essence, the gospel isn't about rules. In *The Theology of the Body for Beginners*, Christopher West writes, "The Gospel is meant to *change our hearts* so that we no longer need the rules." A binary understanding of our sexuality (e.g., we can either turn sexual desire on or off at will) does not reflect our created reality. We are gendered beings who live in flesh and blood bodies that are wired for touch and sexual pleasure: something the anything-goes narrative understands all too well.

HOW FAULTY TEACHING AND CULTURAL
CONDITIONING DERAIL US

Regardless of whether we were raised in the extreme abstinence movement, permissive secular culture, or some place in between, we all have to sift through layers of cultural conditioning and misguided teaching to determine God's intent for our sexuality. This is true even if we've been married for decades.

Starting in adolescence, culture conditions men and women differently. By the early teen years girls know that if they fail to keep their boyfriends sexually satisfied, it's their fault if the boys go elsewhere. I remember standing around a bonfire at a high school pep rally within earshot of an ex-boyfriend. With his arms wrapped around his new crush, he said, "I used to go out with her," nodding in my direction. His girlfriend asked, "Why did you break up with her?" He replied, "She didn't give out." With just four words he effectively shamed me and clarified his expectations for her. I wish I could say that this line of thinking stops when we reach adulthood, but I've heard more than a few male pastors and leaders blame wives for their husbands' sexual indiscretions.

Many Christian women often find themselves in a double bind. Not only are we seemingly responsible for keeping our husbands sexually satisfied, but we're also apparently responsible for mankind's sexual sobriety. Soon after the late Rev. Billy Graham began his public ministry, he, along with several of his trusted friends, decided to safeguard the ministry by implementing several rules, one of which stated that they would not meet individually with a woman unless a third party was present. Known as the "Billy Graham rule," this has become standard practice for many male Christian leaders.

Fidelity should be a nonnegotiable component of marriage, and men are wise to understand their vulnerabilities. But when a male leader refuses to meet one-on-one with a woman, the woman can feel that the man is not safe—and somehow it's her fault. If a man believes that he should never be alone with a woman in a professional or ministerial setting, he's viewing women primarily as objects to be desired rather than as image bearers and co-laborers. Furthermore, such legalistic practices limit women's access to leadership.

Whether it's in the context of one-on-one relationships or in the church at large, women often receive the message that our bodies are both powerful and dangerous. To minimize this and protect our brothers, there's tangible pressure for us to go beyond appropriate modesty and become almost asexual by concealing curves, cleavage, or any other sensual body parts. From this vantage point it can feel like women are perceived to be seductresses who sing their siren songs for the sole purpose of luring unsuspecting men into the rocks, à la Homer's *Odyssey*. While some women do misuse their sexuality and self-objectify, the meta-message here is that men are powerless to resist—which is not at all consistent with Jesus' example or his teachings (see Matthew 5:30).

Secular culture further devalues and dehumanizes women by idolizing their bodies. The fashion and entertainment industries, which serve as baseline indicators of secular beliefs, seem intent on exposing as much female flesh as possible: not to celebrate women's beauty but to sell things. (Men can also be objectified, as shows like *The Bachelorette* prove.)

Though it looks different, cultural conditioning can be similarly unhelpful for men. Throughout their lives, men receive the message that they are wired to constantly think about sex and that their worth is deeply tied to their virility and sexual prowess.

Emphasizing and esteeming virility or frequency encourages men to prioritize the act of sex (which can take less than ten minutes) over intimacy (which takes inestimably longer). This also contributes to the lie that men cannot consistently control their sexual desires. Based on his experiences, Christopher feels that

American culture tends to frame sexual performance as the masculinity litmus test. Even within Christian circles it seems that we're not true men unless we're thinking about having sex all the time. (I think this is more about cultural conditioning and poor anxiety management than anything else.) That the average American male has to exert significant energy to *not think* about sex is a fact: that doesn't mean it's not possible or that we shouldn't develop this ability.

We can't and shouldn't always be thinking about sex. There's too much else to do! The pressure to perform sexually may cause some men to eroticize all of their emotional and physical needs, and some to shut down because they know they can't keep up. If we're promoting the belief that sex is *the* most important component of marriage, we're telling each other the wrong story. We will serve each other and the community at large better if we understand sexual intimacy as being equally important as connecting emotionally and spiritually with our wives.

If men take in these messages and conclude that their behavior is dependent on what someone else does or doesn't do or that the Holy Spirit is not available to them when they feel tempted, they will fail to develop the self-control necessary to remain faithful in thought and deed. When a man's sexuality has been touched by the power of the gospel, he will be able to have a face-to-face conversation with any woman—even a bikini-clad Miss Universe—and maintain control of his body and his mind. Even if he feels tempted or aroused.

To walk in a holy, healthy sexual ethic we must refute erroneous teaching and recognize when culture is leading us astray. We will also need to acknowledge the power of our God-given sexuality, become aware of our areas of temptation, and find the balance between self-control and sexual expression. Regardless of where our misguided input came from or how long it has been influencing us, midlife can be the time when we come into full alignment with God's purposes for our sexuality.

THE WEIGHTS WE CARRY

Coming into alignment includes breaking free from all expressions of broken sexuality, taking responsibility for the sins we've committed, and finding healing for the sins committed against us. Though entire books have been written to address these topics, I want to briefly focus on two components of this journey: how pornography and shame adversely affect marital intimacy.

Pornography. Pornography is a widely practiced type of sexual addiction. *Pornhub*, the number one pornography site worldwide, estimates sixty-four million visitors every day. That's approximately 1 percent of the world's population. Forty million Americans are regular users, and one in three are women. Twenty percent of men admit to watching porn while at work.

There are complex reasons why people watch pornography. Teens are often driven by hormone-fueled curiosity. Because porn offers the illusion of control while it numbs pain and loneliness, those who feel socially awkward or lonely may believe that it's the best or only option to express their sexuality. Christopher was exposed to pornography in his uncle's garage as a precocious twelve-year-old. Not long after, he got hooked in what became a fifteen-year addiction to pornographic imagery and masturbation. In midlife, if normal aging or unexpected health issues have caused complications in the bedroom, pornography might be seen as a viable remedy. It does offer a powerful and predictable release, but it also has many unintended consequences.

Studies have shown that regular pornography use actually changes the neural pathways in the brain. In *Wired for Intimacy*, William Struthers writes, "Repeated exposure to pornography creates a one-way neurological superhighway." On this super-highway the user's "mental life is over-sexualized and narrowed. It is hemmed in on either side by high containment walls making escape nearly impossible."

Pornography and masturbation directly and adversely affect marital intimacy on multiple levels. Pornography stunts our imaginations. There's nothing left to imagine because the images provide everything needed for arousal and orgasm, making us more passive and less creative when it comes to being intimate with our spouse. Pornography and masturbation also prevent us from bonding with each other. They are isolating behaviors that channel our sexual desires away from the marriage bed and leave us with erotic imagery of random men and women.

Because "pornography portrays men and women as objects for our consumption," we learn to dehumanize the object of our desire. There's no reason to consider who these brothers and sisters are or how they might have been coerced to perform. When pornography use is habitual, we're prone to become impatient and unsympathetic with our partner. Why bother with an imperfect, demanding spouse when you can turn to an idealized version of a woman or man who requires nothing of you and can fulfill your fantasies quickly and efficiently?

And finally there's the issue of impulse control. Thanks to 24/7 internet access, having a sexual feeling at 10:05 can result in an orgasm by 10:15. There seems to be no reason to steward our longings—something that's essential for fidelity.

Using pornography and masturbating might be a compelling temptation, but in the long run it renders husbands and wives incapable of loving their spouse wholeheartedly. As is true with any form of idolatry, pornography users are duped into believing that it will fill their needs. In reality, porn leaves men and women trapped, lonely, and ashamed. That's a far cry from what happens when a husband and wife lovingly and freely share their bodies in the marriage bed.

Shame. Shame is another impediment to having a robust, fulfilling sex life. Shame diminishes both our desire and our pleasure. In *Shame and Grace*, Lewis Smedes writes that shame

> is a feeling that we do not measure up and maybe never will measure up to the sorts of persons we are meant to be. . . . The feeling of shame is about our very *selves*—not about some bad thing we *did* or *said* but about what we *are*. Totally. It tells us we are unworthy. It's not as if a few seams in the garment of our selves need stitching; the whole fabric is frayed.

Shame whispers, "If they only knew who you really are, what you did, and what goes on in your head, no one would want to be with you." This deep sense of unworthiness leads us to conclude that others will not and cannot love us and compels us to hide our flaws.

We get a glimpse of how shame attaches to our sexuality via Adam and Eve. After they ate the forbidden fruit, they covered their genitalia with fig leaves. They didn't cover their mouths or their hands, which were directly involved with picking and eating the fruit. Perhaps shame uniquely attaches to our sexuality because sexuality is at the core of who we are. This helps to explain why the purity culture's approach was so effective.

Sexual shame can attach to us via sins that have been foisted upon us (e.g., sexual abuse) as well as our own transgressions (e.g., pornography use). Regarding the former, in a marriage where one (or both) partners have survived trauma or some form of sexualized abuse, developing a satisfying intimate life will take intentionality and a unified effort. Abuse survivors must have their boundaries respected (a no *must* mean no), and may need extra patience and tenderness as they learn how to be vulnerable in a safe relationship. Seeing a professional therapist who specializes in sexual abuse will be beneficial.

If your spouse struggles with shame, one of the most profound gifts you can give them is to regularly remind them that they are fearfully and wonderfully made and that you love them despite their imperfections. In his book *The Mystery of Marriage*, Mike Mason explains that "one of the most fundamental and important tasks that has been entrusted to marriage is the work of reclaiming the body for the Lord, of making pure and clean and holy again what has been trampled in the mud of shame."

This long-term reclamation project is incredibly important in all seasons of life but especially now because many of us feel at odds with our rapidly changing bodies. As we love our spouse with full awareness of their histories, limitations, and scars, shame will lose its grip, freeing us to fully give and receive each other's affection. That's been Michael's experience as he and his wife have gently exfoliated the shame that had been clinging to him.

⸺ ⚭ ⸺

Can you talk more about the shame and pain that you experienced as a result of the purity culture teaching?

MICHAEL The shame I carried and still carry when expressing myself sexually was powerful. After a make-out session with my fiancée when I was twenty-three, I would go back to my house and feel like I must repent, but it was just an amorphous bad feeling. I would take that shame to God, but now I realize it was a massive adventure in missing the point. It took years for me to internalize that God created sex and that he called it good.

130 | MARRIAGE IN THE MIDDLE

How did this shame affect your intimate life after you got married?

MICHAEL   I was a virgin when married at age twenty-four, mostly
as a result of purity culture ethos. It has been special
to cultivate my sexual life with my wife. There is a sa-
credness that has been powerful, especially since she
too was a virgin at marriage. But there was also a very,
very steep learning curve to get to really good sex (for
both of us), which is still ongoing. The sexual shame
contributed to issues with premature ejaculation. Also
it prevented my wife and me from exploring new
sexual behaviors that were off-limits because of ignorance and fear. Even in the context of marriage, purity
culture teaching makes sex more clinical and less juicy
than it actually is.

How did the purity culture teaching affect you long-term?

MICHAEL   This teaching has been deeply disappointing and damaging. I have come to fully reject it, but sorting out the
baby from the bath water has been laborious for my
marriage, intellect, and emotions. Spiritually, it has
been scary. When you are taught that sex has the
power to destroy, changing that perspective is deeply
unnerving—like looking over the edge of a cliff to see
if there's really another path.

Throughout this process I've had to navigate
feeling rebellious, unfaithful, sinful, and rejected even
though years later I can recognize that I wasn't any of
those things.

My sexual-shame residue postmarriage from purity
culture was dual-natured. On the one hand, I was now
married, and sexual expression, according to the
teaching, was supposed to transform from "always sin"

to "must embrace." So the cognitive/intellectual barrier was immediately gone. On the other hand, I was left with lots of responsibility and no physical or emotional skills to handle my sexuality. I'm still working on it. Becoming sexually vulnerable is hard, especially confidently articulating my sexual needs, desires, and fantasies. I wish the coaching I received as an adolescent would have invited me to see those things as gifts, not liabilities.

As you look back, can you see anything that was helpful about the purity movement?

MICHAEL The purity culture's ban on sexuality did help me focus on athletics, friendships, academics, and spiritual life. I accomplished more because I wasn't chasing sex, and girls trusted me much more than they otherwise would have if they felt like I was on the hunt. But I think I also confused and hurt girls in the process since my behavior made them think I was interested, but I never followed through.

How would you have been better served by the church or your youth group?

MICHAEL As a result of the purity movement's shaming and negligence, Christian youth explore sex via pornography. The average porn video is a poor education tool as it describes what should be mutual sexual encounters principally through the male gaze. Continual, long-term shepherding is needed.

I wish the church had offered a strong and regular affirmation of the powerful goodness of sex and sexual expression. That could have included sex education in the context of youth group instead of public school. A theology of the body. Focusing on what it means that God was incarnate. Teaching about the way sex is used in mainstream culture to manipulate and market. I would have been served by three hundred, five-minute conversations across the first twenty years of my life. The one and done approach gave me an orientation but very little knowledge or shepherding. Nobody learns lessons that way.

⌒⌒

If marital sexuality is meant to foster intimacy and afford us pleasure, we must humbly acknowledge when this is not happening and pursue healing. Debra Hirsch sagely observes,

> Our sexuality is indeed a powerful force. It can lead us to something of an experience of either heaven or hell, depending on our ability to orient it toward God or not. This is why it not only needs to be understood and integrated in our spirituality, but also handled with great care—and why it's imperative for Christians to talk more openly about it.

As we reclaim God's purposes for our sexuality, we will discover the beauty and the goodness of our bodies and our sexual desires.

GOING DEEPER

1. What meta-messages or beliefs about sex and sexuality did you bring into your marriage? How do they affect your marriage today?

2. If you came into marriage carrying any shame about your body or about sexuality in general, where did it come from? What triggers shame? What happens to you when you feel shame? What would it take for you to be naked with your spouse and feel no shame?

3. How did you steward your sexuality before marriage? What does stewarding your sexuality look like now, in midlife?

4. Is there anything that limits your freedom and pleasure in the bedroom? If so, what do you think it would take to not be bound by these constrictions?

CHAPTER NINE

SEX, PART 2

Where We Are Now

Helena and Craig had been married for fifteen years when she finally found the courage to reveal her secret: she had been sexually abused by a family member for several years when she was a young teen.

Craig remembers sitting on the bed together when Helena told him. "Thoughts flooded my mind including, *Oh! That explains things.* Then, *Wow! I must be a crappy husband that it took this long for her to trust me. And I'm a pastor!*"

"Things" referred to Helena's disinterest in having sex—particularly for the first five years of their marriage.

They've been married for more than three decades and now have a fulfilling intimate life. This did not happen overnight; it was a long and, at times, frustrating process. Rather than giving up during the intervening years, they both held on to the hope that God not only cared about their intimate life but wanted to help them transform it.

Craig and Helena's experience demonstrates God's advocacy in all aspects of marriage. It also counters the prevailing narrative that sex goes downhill as we age. Our bodies might be softer, slower, and scarred, but they're still capable of experiencing profound pleasure. We may make love less frequently, but when we do, there's more nuance and depth because true intimacy depends more on trust and sacrifice than technique or defined abs.

Reality might be a bit more complicated for others of us. Our sexual histories can sometimes turn into adhesions that constrict us. Cancer or other long-term health issues may have barged into our bedrooms. Ongoing addictions might be diverting sexual energy away from our marriages and creating shame barriers.

With an awareness that this topic can pose just as many challenges as blessings, chapter nine will present a theology of sex and flesh out seven essential characteristics for healthy intimacy. When we fully grasp God's creative intent for our sexuality and then align our thoughts and habits with his design, sex will grow more fulfilling with each passing year.

BIBLICAL SEXUALITY

Because God designed all of creation to reveal himself to us, the marriage covenant and marital sexuality can help us understand God more fully. Psychologist Juli Slattery boldly states, "Of all the things God has created on earth to teach us about His character, none is more powerful in creation or pervasive in Scripture than the marital covenant and the place of sexuality within it. . . . Sexuality is a holy metaphor of a God who invites us into covenant with Himself." If we hope to grasp this truth more fully, we need to differentiate God's intention from the world's narrative. Through objectification and commodification, the world simultaneously worships and demeans the human body. By God's design, the body reflects our Creator and functions not as a marketing tool but as an imperfect yet beautiful container for both the Holy Spirit and human life.

The world inflates the importance of sex but then largely makes it about individual pleasure and, in the process, misses the deeper meaning. Sex is not designed to simply be a momentary act of pleasure between two consenting adults. God intends for sex to be an essential component of a covenanted marriage that draws two people into deeper emotional and spiritual intimacy even as it brings profound pleasure. Rather than being inherently carnal and self-centered, God's design elevates conjugal love as a symbol of Christ's union to the church, making sex both spiritual and sacrificial. In fact, when we prioritize our spouse's needs and make love with an awareness of the Holy Spirit's presence, it results in sex that's truly transcendent.

Again and again, God flips the world's paradigm upside down and inside out. And in the process, he reveals something of his nature and his eternal purposes through marital intimacy. Taking all of this into account, we can discover seven characteristics of sexual intimacy: oneness, mutuality, sacrifice, respect/honor, vulnerability, pleasure, and healing/restoration.

Oneness. Oneness is both mysterious and straightforward—spiritual but also physical. The theme of oneness is prevalent throughout Scripture. For the Jewish people, morning and evening prayer services begin with what's known as the *Shema*: "Hear, O Israel: the LORD our God, the LORD is one" (Deuteronomy 6:4 NIV). Perhaps hinting at the Trinity where all three persons maintain their individuality and yet function as one being, God designed marriage and marital intimacy to join together two distinct individuals who never lose their own identity and yet as a team become something more. This is most obvious in the act of sexual intercourse. As our bodies fit together, they are responding to an ancient call. That call is not base or animalistic but spiritual and heavenly.

The desire to make love—to attain oneness—is a reflection of being created in the image of a relational God. Though genital sex is not the only way to achieve oneness, we are meant to experience unparalleled connection with our spouse through intercourse. In *Embracing the Body*, Tara Owens shares a letter written by the man who would become her husband as he anticipated their physical union:

Making love is creating unity. . . . A husband and wife have been unified—have been made one already—but need to reestablish unity between them. They need to repair what has been broken. . . . They need to reunite with their minds, hearts, wills, and bodies. . . . Making love is creating oneness.

Additionally, incarnate oneness foreshadows God's ultimate plan to unify Christ and the church. Theologian Gerald Hiestand explains, "Drawing upon the ancient marriage formula of Genesis 2:24, Paul reveals that sexual oneness within marriage was created by God *from the beginning*, to serve as a typological foreshadowing of the spiritual oneness that has now begun to exist between Christ and his church—a oneness that has eternally existed in God's intent." Hiestand goes on to say that the way marriage embodies the gospel isn't coincidental but rather "full of divine intentionality." Understanding oneness as both spiritual and physical adds layers of dimensionality to our intimate lives.

Mutuality. When the apostle Paul introduced the idea of marital sex being mutual, it was revolutionary. At that time women were seen as subservient and were expected to satisfy men's needs, sexual and otherwise. Writing to the early Corinthian church, Paul advises that, "The husband should fulfill his wife's sexual needs, and the wife should fulfill her husband's needs. The wife gives authority over her body to her husband, and the husband gives authority over his body to his wife" (1 Corinthians 7:3-4). The goal of mutuality in the bedroom was and continues to be a radical departure from many cultural norms.

Early on in our marriage, Christopher and I decided that we would not be intimate unless both of us wanted to be. That's not to say that there haven't been nights when one of us responds to an invitation with something along the lines of "That's not really my top priority at the moment, but sure." Our practice might mean that we have sex less frequently than some couples, but when we do, we're both totally present and committed to pleasuring each other.

I've had many candid conversations about sex during my twenty-plus years of pastoral care work where women have shared their frustrations and explained why they sometimes grow disinterested in sex.

Because experiencing sexual pleasure and having an orgasm are more mysterious and less linear for women—particularly post-menopause—sex requires a significant physical and emotional commitment. After fulfilling all of their professional and/or family responsibilities on a given day, women may feel making love requires more of them than they have to give. Christopher is perhaps better suited than I am to help men understand this:

> Men, we will experience richer, deeper, more fulfilling sex with our wives if we don't push them or expect sex more frequently than they are able to engage. Women are often labeled as selfish or stubborn if they show any disinterest. There's typically a lot more going on.
>
> It takes most women's bodies a minimum of fifteen minutes of foreplay to be physically ready for intercourse. Unlike men, sexual intimacy demands a level of physical, emotional, and mental focus that cannot be turned on like a spigot. Quick sex is rarely satisfying, often uncomfortable—especially in midlife—and can result in women feeling used.
>
> With regard to frequency, if we feel a compelling need to have an orgasm on a daily basis, it's worth considering whether this is about being overly stressed and not knowing any other strategies to destress. We may have learned in our teen years that the best way to take the edge off of our insecurities was to masturbate before bed. That nightly ritual became fused with sexual pleasure, but its source may have a lot more to do with

self-doubt and anxiety. Our wives are perceptive and will probably feel this disconnect, especially if sex is not really about being with her but about feeling better about ourselves or decompressing from our day. We would do well to consider sex as a form of communication rather than a performance.

If wives have been internalizing and submitting to the perspective that their sexual desires or physical process doesn't matter, by this point discouragement or frustration may eclipse their sense of responsibility, leading them to opt out or simply go through the motions. While understandable, retreating or giving up results in emotional distance and the loss of pleasure.

As with all other areas of life that have been affected by the fall, this dynamic is not beyond redemption. Women (or men if the roles are reversed) will need to reconnect with their sexuality, confess and forgive when necessary, talk about what they need, and commit to reengage. Frustration, hurt, or disappointment—however real—do not give anyone permission to renege on their marriage vows. If you and your spouse feel disconnected or stuck, please consider seeing a licensed therapist.

Sacrificial. Sacrifice deepens and enriches sexual pleasure. I'm guessing that the apostle Paul was probably not thinking about sex when he wrote, "Do nothing from selfish ambition or conceit, but in humility regard others as better than yourselves. Let each of you look not to your own interests, but to the interests of others" (Philippians 2:3-4 NRSV). But this mindset should not be divorced from how we think about and practice sexual intimacy.

To achieve mutuality and oneness, we need to make sacrifices. When I'm in pain or tired at the end of a long day, I'd much rather settle into bed with a book. But fatigue and pain are ongoing issues for me, so as I'm able, I need to push myself and be present to Christopher. On the nights when I can't get around the pain, I ask for a rain check. Sometimes the equation is flipped. In the season when he lost his mom and walked away from a job he loved, Christopher was depressed and mostly disinterested in sex for almost a year. Then I had to steward my sexual desires until he was ready. Our marriage vow should never become a credit card that we swipe at will to get what we want. Instead, our commitment should motivate and empower sacrifice, particularly as we age, because aging can sometimes be cruel.

Like Bill (see chapter 3), Becca had to reckon with how cancer irrevocably transformed her experience of sex. Soon after she discovered a lump in her breast, she had a double mastectomy. Two years later, Becca and her husband are still coming to grips with how profoundly cancer has affected their intimate life.

> My mastectomy threw us for a loop. I think if we had sat down and really thought through how sex would change when I no longer had breasts, we would've had an inkling that there was going to be a struggle ahead, but we were so focused on getting rid of the cancer that losing my breasts was in the periphery.
>
> When I was healed enough to start having sex, it was impossible to do it without confronting the effects of cancer. How do you start over after losing a major erogenous zone?
>
> I found myself wanting to please my husband but being so sad that this was our reality now. He wanted to please me but was cautious about hurting me physically or emotionally. It was really hard. We had multiple attempts that were halted by tears.
>
> For the first few months I always wore a cami during sex. It took a long time to get comfortable with my fake, scarred breasts, and it took a lot of prayer and patience from both of us to get to the point where we are now. We've had to learn new ways to make love. That has involved a lot of honest

communication. When we could accept the reality that sometimes sex would be good and other times not so good, a lot of the pressure was relieved.

Major surgeries and illnesses of this magnitude are bound to disrupt and alter our intimate lives. Becca's cancer necessitated many sacrifices in all aspects of their marriage but perhaps most notably in the bedroom. Because health issues are increasingly common in midlife, lines of communication need to remain open and both partners must refuse to give up.

Honor and respect. Oneness, mutuality, and sacrifice should lead us to respect and honor each other—particularly when we're naked and vulnerable. Christopher believes that

> the measure of our humanity is how we honor each other. I don't presume that my experience is more important or more consequential than Dorothy's. Because she lives with chronic pain, I need to pay attention to how much pain she's experiencing. I don't ever want to exceed what's tolerable. This forces me to be very sensitive and tune in to her. Might that cause me to slow down or adjust? It's all pleasurable, so it does not feel costly to me. By going slower, it honors her and allows for a deeper connection.
>
> If your spouse has had major surgery, if they have been a victim of sexual abuse, the more you honor their story, the more they will feel respected and loved. We don't do this in order to get good sex: we do this because we want to honor our marriage vows and love our spouses well.

We also show honor and respect by loving our spouse's body no matter how much it deviates from cultural norms, personal preferences, or pornographic illusions. Pornography amplifies the discrepancies between reality and our imagination. If we cling to the two-dimensional images and project these fantasies onto our spouse, we diminish them. Far better for us to accept, embrace, and love the whole of our spouse rather than some unrealistic, idealized image.

Midlife is a time when our bodies are rapidly and inextricably changing, sometimes diminishing our sexual desires. We may find ourselves wondering or even fearing whether we'll lose our sexual spark. This might inspire us to try new things. In these situations, share your desires, but make sure you and your spouse are on the same page. Respect and honor should always trump novelty.

Vulnerability. Physical and emotional vulnerability are really about relinquishing control and trusting each other. Any number of issues or feelings can block us from being vulnerable including fear, unresolved anger, resentment, or infidelity. Feeling ashamed about our aging bodies can also incline us to hide or hold back. As one friend quipped, "This is not the body I brought to my husband on our wedding night." That's probably true for many of us.

While it may be difficult to fully give of ourselves if we don't feel at peace with our bodies, choosing vulnerability in light of our insecurities will help us move toward each other. Mike Mason observes,

> To be naked with another person is a sort of picture or symbolic demonstration of perfect honesty, perfect trust, perfect giving and commitment. . . . Exposure of the body in a personal encounter is like the telling of one's deepest secret: Afterwards there is no going back, no pretending that the secret is still one's own or that the other does not know.

Although this kind of vulnerability does not come naturally to all of us, we shouldn't assume it's out of reach. We may need to actively refute self-hatred or recommit to care for our bodies. Whatever it takes, however long it takes, appreciating and loving our bodies will translate to more fulfilling sexual intimacy.

Pleasure. God's meticulous design of the human body offers compelling evidence that he cares about pleasure. Human beings are literally wired for pleasure. Skin is the largest organ and houses millions of touch receptors. One fingertip has more than three thousand nerve endings! Touch is the first sense to develop (in utero) and typically the last sense we lose in the aging process. Our spouse's tender touch stimulates nerve receptors on the surface of our skin but also the production of oxytocin, known as the cuddle hormone. As our lips meet and our fingers brush over each other's erogenous zones, our bodies experience small bursts of pleasure that intensify longing and incline us toward each other.

Orgasm lifts us up and out of our everyday reality. In its purest form, lovemaking between a wife and husband should be both bonding and transcendent. If I had to compare it to anything else, it would be worship. Not the rote singing of a half-awake congregation but the Hallelujah chorus-like moments when the Holy Spirit's presence is palpable. We need this kind of transcendence, particularly as we age. It fosters an anticipation of heaven and allows us to let go of our frustrations, disappointments, and losses.

Healing and restoration. Sexual intimacy is meant to serve as an agent of healing in marriage. If we learn to understand every act of lovemaking as a reaffirmation of our marriage vows, our *yes!* not only bonds us together but becomes a healing balm for our lover's deepest wounds. Touch and intercourse allow us to bind up each other's broken hearts and speak life into each other's dry bones.

Being an agent of healing in our marriage requires sustained patience, gentleness, and faithfulness. When our partner's injuries are slow to heal, we may grow impatient or weary. That's understandable, but we can't rush healing or force it to happen in our time frame. (And the deeper the wound and the longer it has gone unaddressed, the more time healing takes.) If we try to hurry the process, it may have the opposite effect. When we assure our spouse of our unconditional love and affirm that we're not going anywhere, we create the kind of environment that facilitates healing and restoration.

MEETING IN THE MIDDLE

With regard to sex, aging tends to rearrange the plus and minus columns. For most of us, frequency has dropped from multiple times per week in the peak years to once a week or less. Some couples may discover that having sex once a month fulfills them. Determining a pace that's satisfactory to both partners can become particularly complicated during midlife due to any number of extenuating circumstances such as fluctuating hormones and sleep issues. It's wise to regularly check in, adjust when necessary, and resist comparing our pace to anyone else's. That said, long gaps without sexual intimacy can leave us disconnected and vulnerable. If it's been more than six months and there are no extenuating health issues, talk about what's going on and reach out for help.

Midlife sex is affected by many factors, including how aging alters our bodies' responses to foreplay and stimulation. Once I started perimenopause, the familiar process that my body followed from arousal to orgasm became perplexing and unpredictable. This required Christopher to pay attention to subtleties and sometimes exhibit great patience. Occasionally, sex is over in twenty minutes, and sometimes it takes more than an hour. This modicum of uncertainty about how my body will respond can become an impediment to initiating sex. If it's past nine p.m., I have to ask myself, *Do I have an hour of aerobic activity in me?* My spirit is generally willing, but these days, my flesh is often tired.

Passing through menopause liberates women from birth control but requires them to address the unpleasant issue of vaginal dryness. (Coconut oil works great.) And on the other side of the bed, men may struggle with erectile dysfunction, which can be as shameful as it is disconcerting. If ED becomes a factor in midlife sex, couples can learn how to pleasure one other without intercourse and even without having an orgasm. ED might require renegotiating the terms, but it should not end sexual intimacy.

Making love is inextricably connected to and dependent on how we're doing emotionally and spiritually. "Sex is one of those mysteries that, like prayer, will not yield to technique, and any approach with a view to technical mastery will be doomed from the start. What the sex life really demands is the loving gift of the self, the sincere devotion of the whole heart." Essentially, the goal is for us to go forward to get back to the Garden. To be naked and unashamed. To offer the whole of who we are to our beloved.

The process of honoring each other with our bodies is work. Sometimes we get tired or sloppy in our praxis. The temptation to give up or look outside of our marriage will always exist. By staying engaged and continuing to value sexual intimacy, marital sex will be a good gift rather than an onerous obligation. Craig and Helena's story offers a compelling example of what's possible when we trust God for more and continue to do our work.

-᠎ᢀᢁᢀ-

Tell me about the first few years of your marriage and this conflict around sex.

HELENA   I didn't really want sex. It was hard for me to even express any kind of affection because I never saw it in my house growing up. I closed up when he wanted touch.

CRAIG   I was a virgin and in my roaring twenties. This is what I'd been waiting for and then I felt almost as if I had to beg for sex, which got me angry. I thought, *This is crazy.* Then when we did make love, she was not able to have an orgasm during intercourse. It was really tough. I mean really, really, really tough.

HELENA   It was tough for me too. I would always be thinking, *What's wrong with me?* It wasn't so much shame but frustration. I remember saying, "Why did you marry me? You could have married someone better!"

CRAIG   As I've gotten older, I've looked back at how many times I probably could've messed up my life with regard to stepping outside of our marriage for sex. It was the grace of God. I don't mean there were close calls, but there was grace that there wasn't really anything in my mind that said, *You know what? I've had enough of this.* My lack of acting out was the grace of God.

HELENA   I married the right man. I'm sure another man would've been gone. Long gone.

How did you make it through? Did you go to counseling or talk with other couples about what was going on?

CRAIG   Once we started dating, we established a weekly day of fasting and prayer. Prayer has always been a huge part of our relationship. Our prayer time has changed over the years, but generally speaking we try to make sure that we spend at least five minutes each day praying together. We share what God has been saying to us or what's been on our hearts. Then we simply pray about those things.

HELENA   We stood on Hebrews 11:6, which ends with, "God rewards those who diligently," meaning constantly, persistently, and unrelentingly, "seek Him" (NKJV). And he certainly did just that for us. Our fasting was based on Isaiah 58: Fasting looses the bands of wickedness, lets the oppressed go free, and breaks every yoke, as in bondage. God promised freedom and guidance and that's how we made it out of those first five years.

CRAIG I also read a lot of books. We were fortunate that around the time we got married, there were godly men writing and talking about this. I learned that many women don't have an orgasm during intercourse. So I realized that what was going on for us was not abnormal. It was more like what we are seeing on television, where both partners have quick, simultaneous orgasms, was a lie.

HELENA Craig's patience helped me to peel off the layers of hurt. I felt safe with him and I knew he was going through it with me. I know he was praying for me and kept telling me, "I see your potential. I see who you can be." Hearing that helped me to heal. We also both knew God called us to be married.

Helena, what prompted you to tell Craig about the abuse after all those years?

HELENA I had a thought one day and knew it was the Holy Spirit. I didn't want to hide anything from him. I felt I needed to share this with him, and this was the right time. When I did, a burden was definitely lifted from me. This facilitated healing and allowed me to be more open and free with Craig. The Holy Spirit kept speaking to me and saying, *It's okay to be his wife. If you let me help you, it's going to be okay.* Gradually, I just started opening up.

What advice would you give to a couple in your church who came to you saying they're struggling with their intimate life?

HELENA I know it sounds cliché, but I would definitely tell them to try and make prayer, talking to God together, a vital part of their healing. And also find support.

CRAIG   I've really become more aggressive in saying to couples, "Don't hide stuff." I would advocate for getting help. I see us as outliers. Our journey is not for everyone. We really didn't get any help. Helena eventually talked with a therapist, but that was late in the game.

 We have to be very careful to not mix our story with a theory. What I mean by that is our route could mess with your route. I think our journey is a miraculous one.

 I was recently with a few younger married men, and as a guy who was heading into his sixties, I was signaling, "Hey, let me tell you something. If you think sex is good now, you haven't seen anything yet. Trust me. You'll be even happier if you hang in there." I want to help folks understand sex does not go downhill as we grow older.

What's your intimate life like now?

HELENA   It's fulfilling. I feel more freedom. I can be naked and unashamed. I feel like I don't need to hold back anymore, and I'm even able to initiate at times. Pleasing him really gives me a great sense of accomplishment.

CRAIG   Bless the Lord! [Craig then looks over at Helena and says,] "I'm having dual thoughts here. I was actually hoping we might go home and . . ." [He raises his eyebrows and laughs.]

Sexual intimacy helps us understand how a covenanted relationship fosters liberated passion. Numerous studies have shown that married couples rank the highest in sexual satisfaction. Even though this contradicts the cultural narrative, it's not surprising. From within the safety of our marriage and empowered by the Holy Spirit, we can choose to fully and freely give ourselves over to God's creative intent. And it is so very good.

GOING DEEPER

1. What's your understanding of God's intention for married sex? Are you and your spouse on the same page with regard to foreplay, frequency, and pleasure? If not, spend some time discussing your differences and figuring out how you might move toward each other.

2. Of the seven characteristics listed, where would you like to grow? What might that growth involve?

3. With regard to your intimate life, what's working? What's not working? If there are any disappointments, frustrations, or unresolved conflicts in your marriage, how are they affecting your intimate life?

4. How has midlife changed sex? In what ways have the physical and emotional changes been blessings? In what ways have they posed challenges?

5. What does it mean to honor your spouse with your body? How could you be more attentive to your spouse's sexual needs?

CHAPTER TEN

COMMUNITY

We'll Get by with a Little—
or a Lot—of Help from Our Friends

Jonathan and Ruth were both single and fresh out of college when they joined a large, metropolitan church. After ministering together for a few years, they started dating and married the following year.

Their church involvement quickly increased. "There was no ministry that we did not take part in," Ruth admits. "We rarely said no to anything. I counted my life a loss for the sake of the gospel. Looking back, I realize we had no boundaries."

That lack of boundaries combined with their desire to please those in authority eventually became an issue. At the time, Ruth and Jonathan did not realize that their church relied on a controlling, hierarchical structure that often prioritized the church's goals over the parishioners' needs.

Jonathan explains, "The church was growing quickly. The only way for the leadership to keep it codified was to become more controlling." Members were expected to unilaterally submit to their leaders' directives in every area of their life, including how they spent their time and who they spent their time with. The combination of controlling leaders with high expectations and members who were culturally conditioned to submit to and respect those same leaders created the perfect setup for what happened next.

When Ruth was home alone, one of the church's pastors came to their house on the pretense of a church matter. Once inside, he molested her. She was shocked and reported the event to the leadership. They urged her not to tell anyone—even Jonathan. And she didn't. For sixteen years.

During that same season, Ruth and Jonathan continued to meet their many church commitments while working full time and parenting young children. "We were exhausted and burned out. We were coexisting in our marriage. The leaders knew this, but their marriages were in trouble too. I wanted to leave but believed that if we left the church, we would be backsliding. So we stayed and kept quiet." Several years later they did leave, but by that point, significant damage had been done.

Some couples would have given up on the church after going through an experience like this. Though deeply hurt, Jonathan and Ruth knew they could not sustain a healthy marriage unless they had intimate friendships and were part of a larger community. Less than a decade after breaking away from this organization, they are now leading in a vibrant, healthy church where they are respected, appreciated, and loved.

It is tempting to minimize the difficult parts in Jonathan and Ruth's story. Unfortunately, painful relational experiences (inside and outside of church) are not aberrations. By this point, most of us have been abandoned, betrayed, or used, leaving us wondering if we should give up on community and friendships—or at least lower the bar. If we refuse to talk about what happened and how we have been hurt, we won't heal. And if we don't heal, we may be relationally impaired for the remainder of our lives.

Midlife reveals a fundamental truth of creation: it really isn't good for us to be alone. Studies show that friendships are not only integral to our mental and physical well-being but also to the health of our marriage. Friends ease our aloneness, provide for our needs, and become the proving ground for love, all of which strengthen our marriages. Though it's true that we're wounded in relationship, it's also true that we can find healing and life-giving support there too.

A WORD ON FRIENDSHIP IN THE TWENTY-FIRST CENTURY

When most of us were growing up, community and friendship were more narrowly defined. The former was limited to the people who lived in close proximity. Our nuclear families were likely to be within a one-day drive. Friendship circles were composed of classmates, neighbors, and possibly a few out-of-state cousins. In today's hyperconnected world, things have changed—particularly for those of us living in metropolitan areas.

According to Facebook, I have 1,250 "friends." I've only met half of them face-to-face. It's virtually impossible to manage the ever-expanding relational circles without engaging in a form of social Darwinism. To bring order, we now categorize relationships into hierarchies based on any number of criteria such as close friend versus mere acquaintance, religious beliefs, membership in common organizations, or shared interests such as kombucha brewers with a sense of humor. (I did not make that up.)

This kind of rating system didn't exist when friendships depended on proximity or blood ties. Back then—before we were all bewitched by social media—we worked harder to maintain friendships because our options were limited. Today, our seemingly limitless options coupled with the ease of unfriending encourage us to function as if friends are expendable.

We also spend increasing amounts of time forming and nurturing relationships online. These points of connection can be meaningful and sometimes develop into rich friendships. But the hours spent in front of a screen can also render us unavailable to the neighbor across the street or the spouse living under the same roof. I'm a total fan of technology, but it can feel like a constant battle to keep it from taking over my life.

THE PROMISE OF HEALTHY COMMUNITIES AND HEALTHY FRIENDSHIPS

For both single and married Christians, church communities often become one of the most significant and influential places for us to connect. Gathering on a weekly basis unifies and strengthens us even as it helps us to transcend our many differences. As we join our voices together in song and prayer, partake of Communion, and engage in kingdom work, we become part of something bigger than ourselves.

Though church communities provide excellent opportunities for us to connect and support each other, they will never be perfect. Because of this reality, we have to forbear and forgive—but also be willing to recognize and name any unhealthy or dysfunctional dynamics. This is complicated. It's not always easy to gauge a church's health on Sunday mornings when all we have to go on are somewhat superficial metrics and personal preferences: Is the worship leader appropriately hip but not outside my comfort zone? Is the preacher affable, witty, and relevant? Are the chairs comfortable? Do they serve fair trade coffee with nondairy creamer in recyclable cups? It's totally natural that certain strategic choices appeal to our sensibilities and others offend us. However, we need to dig a bit deeper because *there's a lot at stake in this choice.* It's not simply about how we spend a few hours every Sunday morning.

If a church is led by leaders who value maturity and wholeness (rather than the *appearance* of maturity and wholeness), that community will help to support and sustain healthy marriages and healthy families. Conversely, being part of a toxic community makes us vulnerable to sin and marital failure. The churches that Jonathan and Ruth and Scot and Camille (chapter 2) attended were broken from the top down. Rather than coming alongside these couples in their time of need, church leaders created a wedge between the spouses. If you're currently part of a religious or secular community that silences questions, disregards boundaries, or ignores cries for help, prayerfully consider whether it would be wise to move on.

Healthy communities and healthy friendships are unique to time, place, and culture but have three fundamental traits—all of which play a pivotal role in strengthening our marriages: honest accountability, diversity, and willingness to suffer together.

Accountability. Within church settings, accountability is an overused word and an underutilized concept. At the core, accountability is "proactive honesty." Where confession is an honest admission of failure after the fact, accountability aims to prevent us from falling. If we want healthy marriages, healthy friendships, and healthy communities, we can't dodge or obfuscate the truth. That does not mean that we should haul off and express every stray thought that drifts through our mind. (There's Twitter for that.) Passionate feelings or opinions are often simply passionate feelings and opinions, not the gospel truth. We must find the balance between discerning which thoughts and feelings should be shared and with whom. If someone I barely know asks me how I'm doing, it's not wise for me to divulge the blowup that Christopher and I had the night before. However, if we're having dinner with long-time friends and I respond to that question with "We're good!" that's a problem.

Part of what drives our temptation to hide our weak or broken places is that we live in an age when image ranks as one of the most important measures of success. Thank you, social media. Many of us feel the need to curate our public persona and give off the impression that we've got everything figured out. When we place a high value on others' opinions of us, we will naturally be tempted to cover up our imperfections. We may assume that if we admit we're drowning in debt or haven't made love in more than a year that others will judge us. The truth is, they might. Honesty is risky. But if we only let others see our strengths, we're never going to be fully known. And we need to be fully known—both inside and outside of marriage.

For that to happen, others need to see us when we're not our best selves. It's easy to report on a rough patch after the fact when there's no danger of feeling vulnerable. It's quite different to call a friend and say, "My husband and I are not doing well. Could we hang out and talk this weekend?" Or "I need you to come over immediately because I'm afraid I might hurt our kids." (Actual quote said by me to my neighbor one afternoon when I was exhausted and short-tempered.) Honest vulnerability dismantles our façades. When our friends then love us even after witnessing our meltdowns and recalcitrant behaviors, we can trust that their love is genuine. That kind of unconditional love helps us to heal and mature. It also helps to prevent moral failure.

Maybe one reason we resist accountability is that we fail to see it as a normal, essential ingredient of relationship. When we hold this perspective, accountability can become artificial. My friend Brad Wong, a pastor in the Bay Area, believes that "accountability can be an external pressure rather than internalized ownership." If we incorporate this kind of proactive honesty in our friendships, we will naturally confess our sins and admit where we need help—including in our marriages.

Another reason the concept of accountability often falls short is that we tend to assume that when we ask someone to hold us accountable, it's partially their fault if we fall. Others can play a definite role in helping us to make good choices, but we are solely responsible for our thoughts and behaviors.

As an example of proactive accountability, if you realize that you tend to gripe about your spouse in a particular friendship circle, the next time you're together you could say, "I'm struggling to love my husband well and my complaining is not helping. If I start griping, please tell me to stop." Like the mortification that happens when we confess, voicing our vulnerabilities clarifies our contribution to any issues and helps us to find solutions. If your friends or accountability partners never follow through, you can do one of three things: convince yourself that you're fine and don't really need help, reiterate your request, or ask someone else. When we practice proactive honesty, it not only changes us but can also change everyone around us.

Many years ago married friends of mine revealed that they were in a difficult space. At that time I was a single woman and felt disqualified from entering their fray. But because they invited me into their struggle, I challenged the husband to consider how his choices were affecting his wife. About a decade later my friend recounted how that conversation had been pivotal for them. They've now been together for more than thirty-six years. I'm not taking credit for the longevity of their marriage, but I do believe there are times when we need to risk offending our friends for the sake of helping them see what they may not see on their own.

Accountability is also needed in the community at large. As Ruth and Jonathan's story illustrates, because we're broken human beings who create flawed systems, we desperately need transparent accountability on the corporate level. It's nearly impossible to avoid some type of moral failure without this. Of late, there are far too many cautionary tales of how badly things can go when those in power make poor choices and then try to get away with it. The list of pastors who have recently stepped down due to moral failures reads like a Who's Who of twenty-first-century Christian leaders. In many of these situations, marriages have been torn apart.

When the curtain is finally pulled back, we typically discover that corrupt behavior has been going on for years. No one wakes up one morning and decides, *You know, I feel like embezzling church funds or having an affair or firing all the dissenting voices today.* We cross the line of blatant immorality only after making thousands of incremental steps in that direction.

Proactive accountability can stop or at least slow down the progression of sin, provided that we're willing to let go of our privilege and status. Much heartache and collateral damage might be avoided if board members and church elders valued being accountable to God and their peers rather than protecting their leader's power base.

Moral relativism has made it increasingly difficult to call others to account. When we do, we run the risk of coming off as judgmental or hypocritical. By the time we've reached midlife, most of us have witnessed our friends and our church communities make incredibly stupid mistakes. (And we've probably made a few ourselves.) If we err on the side of shrinking back when we see our friends or leaders acting foolishly or sinfully, in the end we're all going to suffer.

For accountability to be part of a friendship or a community, forgiveness must be practiced. Biblical forgiveness does not exclude holding others accountable or even formally pressing charges. When someone has caused physical injury or broken the law (e.g., incest or misappropriation of funds), the authorities should be notified. There may or may not be tangible consequences, but accountability always moves toward restoration by asking, "What do I need to do to make things right?" As friendships, communities, and marriages faithfully practice this kind of accountability, everyone benefits.

Diversity. There are many metrics for diversity including ethnicity, gender, marital status (single, married, divorced, and widowed), employment (professional, manual laborer, stay-at-home parent, un- or underemployed, etc.), income, education level, and political affiliation. Not many relational circles or communities include such broad representation. However, when homogeneity defines our friendships and faith communities, we need to be aware of the possible consequences.

By excluding those who are different—whether intentionally or unintentionally—our worlds get smaller and we risk stunting our growth. That's because differentness confronts our biases and prejudices. The defensiveness or fear that rises up when someone challenges us or simply doesn't agree with our perspective can actually help us to be kinder and more empathetic provided that we listen and learn rather than react.

Two of our close friends are black. We've had many discussions about issues that most sane people normally avoid—such as how white privilege perpetuates systemic racism. Because they have a distinct vantage point and are committed to speaking the truth, they're not afraid to challenge us on any number of topics, including our marriage. They have helped Christopher and me to see broken relational dynamics that we might otherwise overlook or excuse. Diverse relationships often require more effort, more stretching, and more leaning in, but they pay rich dividends. They enlarge our understanding of God's kingdom and help us to see and value different perspectives.

Though we're all vulnerable to the gravitational pull of sameness, giving in to it becomes problematic, particularly as we age. Calcified opinions and dogmatism might work on talk radio but not in real life. Lately, I've noticed how quickly I can feel annoyed or impatient with people who dismiss or disagree with the issues that matter most to me. In these situations, I find myself wanting to moralize my opinions and retreat to my ideological silo. While that might make my life less conflictual, it will not help me to be a better neighbor—or wife. The choice to withhold love from one person or one type of person becomes like cancer in our heart. That's why it's imperative for us to love and mourn with our enemies.

Suffering together. As all of the interviews in this book reveal, every marriage and every community will experience hardship—no matter how righteous or faith-filled we are. The question isn't whether we'll suffer but how we'll respond when we do. Often, we try to control situations and outcomes rather than submit to the limits of our power. But "if we can believe that God is for us, and ask him to 'make it count' rather than to make it stop, His refining fire will" mature our faith and enable us to offer compassion and comfort to others. Learning how to suffer with your spouse and members of your community is crucial in this time frame because the losses begin to mount.

There are some very real cultural barriers to suffering well. For instance, Anglo-Americans tend to believe in exceptionalism ("we're special") and triumphalism ("we should always victorious"). This perspective leaves no room for pain or loss, which hampers us when we or those we love are suffering. It also inclines us to extend weak platitudes (e.g., "God won't give you more than you can handle") or keep our distance from those who are in pain because we feel awkward or guilty. We don't need to be licensed therapists to support our friends; we simply need to humbly show up and offer compassion.

When this happens, it's beautiful. After Kim Findlay's five-year-old daughter perished in a house fire, a group of close friends literally dropped what they were doing to sit with her. She recalls, "They didn't try to fix it or control me. They let me guide what I could handle." Six years later when her marriage was falling apart, the response from her coworkers was markedly different.

Though she had been on the church staff for fourteen years, none of them reached out to her or her husband. Kim recounts, "I would've loved for them to pray for us: genuine, spirit-filled prayer, not advice-giving disguised as prayer. I never felt we were honored as people with our own stories." Providing comfort and support may require us to keep quiet about our deeply held convictions. In certain situations, we best demonstrate Christ's love simply by being present and entering into another's suffering.

Grieving and lamenting are two of the ways we can do this. While grief is a straightforward expression of pain, "lament is a cry of injustice; it is the piecing howl of protest against evil. . . . It screams that death has wronged us, but it will not have the final say." Christopher and I recently lost three middle-aged friends. I left the third funeral with a fierce headache because I spent two hours clenching my jaw to keep myself from weeping. During the service I debated giving voice to my grief but because I feared no one else would join me and I would make a spectacle of myself, I reined it in.

Lament and public expressions of grief are rarely practiced in the United States, at least in predominately white churches. I'm not sure if that's because we fear losing control or because we believe lament and grief are incompatible with our faith. Scripture reveals that grief and lament are actually God-centric responses to pain and loss. They bear witness to the reality of suffering. When we weep with the husband who just lost his wife of thirty-nine years, we validate his pain. When we mourn with the woman whose husband recently walked out on her, we affirm that we have no intention of abandoning her too. This is powerful and healing.

We can only truly grieve and lament with others when we relinquish our need to control and our impulse to fix. By serving as trustworthy companions and allowing others to lean on our faith, their suffering won't feel so lonely or hopeless. Aubrey Sampson believes, "Lament can lead us back to a place of hope—not because lamenting does anything magical, but because God sings a louder song than suffering ever could."

WHY RELATIONSHIPS MATTER

Sowing into relationships is one of the best decisions that we can make during this season of life when we're constantly facing losses and bumping into our limitations. That's because even the most amazing spouse will not be able to consistently meet all of their partner's needs. Friendships will fill those gaps and, as researchers have been discovering, improve our overall health.

A recent article in the *Wall Street Journal* noted that "loneliness takes a physical toll, and is as closely linked to early mortality as smoking up to fifteen cigarettes a day or consuming more than six alcoholic drinks a day." A longitudinal study done by Harvard University confirms this. In a 2015 TED talk, Professor Robert Waldinger reported it wasn't midlife cholesterol levels that predicted how men were going to age but rather how satisfied they were in their friendships. "The people who were the most satisfied in their relationships at age 50 were the healthiest at age 80."

Once a quarter I have a standing date with three female friends. We've been having meals together for twenty-seven years. We laugh, we cry, we endure poorly made restaurant food, and we pray for each other. They know my strengths and my weaknesses. Their intimate, consistent friendship has brought light and hope into some of my darkest days, and I am truly grateful for them.

There are any number of legitimate reasons why prioritizing friendships in midlife can be tricky, including lack of time and conflicting beliefs (political and otherwise). Regarding the former, we all have many urgent demands pressing on us. So much so that the thought of initiating a meal with friends can feel impossible or even irresponsible. The truth is that we can and should prioritize connecting with friends on a regular basis. Yes, it does require energy and effort. But in the long run, it's well worth it.

As we age, many of us move further east or west on the ideological spectrum. This can test our relationships and make us wonder if our love is strong enough to stretch without snapping. In certain situations it might feel tempting to conclude that the relationship has run its course. When that feeling rises up, take a moment to remember how your friends have shown love and support over the decades and pray for grace because these friendships might be God's provision for whatever lies ahead.

Jonathan and Ruth's story is complex. There's not a simple before and after. Ten years later, they're still processing what happened and how it affected them. Their story highlights what's needed in a community and in friendships for that community or those friendships to have a positive net gain in marriage. If a church community skims the surface and never teaches us how to apply the gospel to our lives, we will be at a disadvantage when a crisis hits. If our friends are unable to listen and support us when we're going through the inevitable challenges, we'll learn to buck up and post smiling family photos on social media like everyone else. Because Jonathan and Ruth wanted more, they were willing to admit "there's something wrong here" and then talk about it. That choice helped them to move toward healing and eventually reengage with the church.

How were you able to gain enough clarity and courage to leave your previous church?

RUTH   Short answer? I was depressed and that depression was not going away, which compelled me to stop being the perfect church member. More specifically, I started doing two things that I loved: running and reading. The latter was an act of rebellion because we had been taught that we should only read Scripture and books they recommended. As I was reading *Boundaries* by Henry Cloud and John Townsend, I started to realize that our church philosophy wasn't the only way to do things. I wondered, *How could I not know this?*

JONATHAN Our cultural background, Asian American, says family is more important than the individual. We were taught not to dishonor our mothers and fathers and not to shame the church or the pastors. Then from the pastors the message we got was obedience, obedience, obedience. Additionally, there was a code of silence. No one was talking about any of the dysfunction, so we assumed we were the only ones who were struggling.

Things were getting worse for us. Ruth and I were very unhappy. We had not been intimate for two to three years. I blamed myself. I thought everything was my fault. I was watching TV every night and telling Ruth I was working late. Then I started reading other books and questioning the church's teaching too. There was one particular book we both read about marriage and I thought, *Wow! What we're going through is not normal.*

RUTH   After I read about boundaries, I started reading on forgiveness. That led me to start thinking about who I needed to forgive, which was messy because our church essentially taught us that "no matter who's at fault, it's your fault." But I wanted to be thorough, so I went through my mental Rolodex of people as far back as I could remember. It was very freeing.

(Around the same time, Ruth and Jonathan, along with several other couples, began a church plant that lasted three years. They then sensed it was time to move on. The next year they took a sabbatical to rest but also to find another church.)

When the time came, what was it like to reengage with church?

RUTH   For the first year we decided that we were not going to sign up for anything. We sat in the last row. We had the itch to do things. We saw needs, and then we'd look at each other and remember, we're not here to meet needs: we're here to meet Jesus.

JONATHAN We also peppered the lead pastor with lots of questions. We wanted to know about the church structure, about their beliefs, and especially about accountability. In our previous church the pastors were not accountable to anyone. The first time I had a question about how things were done in our new church, I decided to share my concern. They heard me and respected me because I spoke up. That builds trust.

In this new church, the pastors are not afraid to share their own struggles and vulnerabilities from the front. That honest vulnerability makes it easier for us to trust them and to know that it's okay to talk about this stuff.

Your previous church was monocultural and friendships were tightly controlled, mostly forming around ministry. Your new church is more racially diverse and much more relaxed about both ministry and friendships. Has it been easy or difficult for you both to forge new friendships given these notable differences and your unique history?

JONATHAN There was a lot of floundering in the beginning. We had to ask a lot of questions: What's our definition of friendship? How do you even form friendships at this stage of life, especially when there's no structure? Does that mean being together 24/7, like in our previous church? And then after asking those questions, we recalibrated based on what we learned.

RUTH Because the old church was so homogenous and because we were all told what to do, there was a cohesive way of relating to each other. It's harder now. We can't control what people do. Connecting takes longer and involves a lot of baby steps. We invite people to our house group, but we can't control who will show up or whether they'll come back.

JONATHAN We're still trying to figure out how much of the closeness we felt at our former church was authentic versus a function of our obedience. At the time it felt real, but as we look back, maybe it wasn't. The friendships that we're forming now are more real because they aren't forced. When people respond, you know they like you, which feels more genuine and more joyful. But, as Ruth said, it's more chaotic, much slower, and very risky.

Ruth, after holding on to the secret for sixteen years about being molested by your pastor, you finally decided to tell Jonathan. Why? And what was that like for both of you?

RUTH Being willing to talk about it was the first real step in my healing. I got together with another woman who had also been part of our old church. She shared that the same pastor had abused her. We both wept. All these years I thought I was the only person. Until that point I wasn't ready to tell Jonathan. Now I felt it was time.

JONATHAN That rocked my world. This guy had been my spiritual father for twenty years. I could finally understand what had been going on in our marriage. We both went through counseling individually and as a couple. It took me a while to accept that it was normal to have so many different feelings like anger and sadness. After a year of processing, we had enough healing to go to the next place.

There's only so much healing you can do on your own. It was only when I was able to trust others and feel accepted by them that deeper healing came. This work had to be done in the body. We were hurt in church, and our healing has come through the church.

Last year when we returned to church after a family vacation, it felt like I came home. That took four years.

Jonathan and Ruth have met with regional overseers in their previous denomination to voice their concerns about the possibility of ongoing abuse. They are also connecting with other couples who have gone through similar experiences to offer them hope and help them find healing.

‑e‑e‑

Though they had ample reason to give up on the church and church people, Jonathan and Ruth chose not to. Their choice embodies this fundamental truth: "The hope of the gospel is that it invites us out of hiding, not to expose us and parade our pain in front of everyone, but to heal it and root us within real community." May the grace of God empower us to live in this complex reality.

GOING DEEPER

1. Do you have at least one other couple you trust and regularly spend time with? If not, what might that be costing you? Are you vulnerable with them? If not, how could you move in that direction?

2. Would you consider spending time with a younger couple in order to support and mentor them? What might that look like?

3. How often do you ask for input or help from people who might disagree with or challenge you? If seldom or never, what might that cost you in the long run?

4. How does your community support marriages? How does it support singles or those who are divorced? If there are gaps, would you consider trying to meet some of those needs?

CHAPTER ELEVEN

TELOS REPRISED

Becoming Marriage Visionaries

I wish I could conclude this book by boasting about how God swiftly and decisively redeemed all of the losses I detailed in the opening chapter. God *has been* redeeming what we lost, but it's not been quick or unequivocal.

In fact, it has taken seven years for us to recover, seven years for Christopher to feel at peace with his vocation, and seven years to find a church home where we're both valued and released to lead. Seven years feels like a long time. Of course, by biblical standards that's little more than the blink of an eye.

As Christopher and I look back on that season, we can now see how God was bringing order out of the chaos all along, even when darkness obscured his presence. While we were freaking out about the bedbugs and trying to accept his mother's staggeringly quick death, our eldest son—the one we had dropped off at college on the ill-fated trip—met the incredible woman who is now his wife. When we walked away from the church we loved, I temporarily lost my context to minister alongside Christopher but began writing. I find this discipline deeply fulfilling, and I doubt that either of my books would exist if we hadn't left.

Christopher's professional journey has been more complex. The fifteen years he spent serving as worship, arts, and healing pastor in a diverse, urban setting were the most vocationally coherent and satis-fying he'd had up to that point. All of his gifts were at play in one place. His crisis of doubt revolved around ageism in the workplace: the gnawing realization that being a worship leader is akin to being a pro athlete. Now in his fifties, he fears he's only welcome on the sidelines or in the booth with a headset—and only as long as his team keeps winning.

Rather than making a lateral shift into another full-time pastoral position, Christopher returned to the calling of his early adulthood: teaching theater to teens and leading worship on the weekends. The rewards are just as rich as they were in his full-time pastoral role, but the focus and energy required to juggle his bivocational life make for exacting days and, at times, wakeful nights. He's mindful that there are no guarantees regarding what's ahead, but having landed on his feet after "God flipped the chessboard," he no longer doubts that he has something to offer the larger world.

One of the lessons from our season of shaking was that having integrity doesn't spare us from pain and loss. Make no mistake: righteous living has definite merits and can protect us from *some* suffering. But a good portion of the pain and loss that we experience in life connects directly to seemingly random occurrences and others' sin. This feels disquieting and unjust. It's troubling to see so many hard-hearted, physically healthy men and women out there wal-lowing in wealth while the righteous wait for bread and healing.

In the early years of parenting, one of our sons frequently as-serted his will by informing us, "You're not the boss of me!" I don't always like this reality, but we're not the boss of God. The anger and bewilderment that we sometimes feel when he refuses to play by our rules exposes our preference to control and our struggle to trust his goodness—especially when circumstances are dire. Though it makes no sense, sometimes fighting against God is easier than submitting to him. It can be terrifying to prostrate ourselves in front of the cross when we don't know what God's next move will be.

Once the shock had worn off and our false paradigms finished unraveling, Christopher and I found ourselves face down before that cross. We were disheveled but still holding on to each other and some remnant of our faith. We both had the same question: *Now what?* We knew we needed to allow the grief and loss to transform us, to make us more like Christ and draw us closer to each other, but we only had a rough outline of what that might look like.

Before the unraveling started, Christopher and I assumed that because we had done so much relational and spiritual work in our thirties and forties we would now be able to sit back and enjoy the fruits of our labor. Apparently, God never signed off on our ten-year plan. Instead of ascending, we were descending. And our exceedingly low vantage point afforded us a new perspective of everything, including our marriage. Nothing exposes a marriage's weak spots quite like sitting at the dinner table with the same person night after night. What we discovered was humbling.

We realized that we frequently overextended ourselves on behalf of those we were leading. So much so that sometimes we only had crumbs to give each other. (This is a common issue for pastors and leaders.) Rather than looking ahead to discern where *our family* wanted or needed to go (our telos), we were imagining where we could take the enterprise. This made us stellar employees but somewhat mediocre spouses and parents. And, yes, it grieves me to acknowledge this, particularly because we cannot get those years back.

Without the external structure that previously held us together and gave us context, we had to find new ways to serve God and support each other. The fact that all of this coincided with two of our parents passing away and all three of our sons moving on made the need to adapt and grow all the more imperative.

In the midst of this upheaval, we learned just how difficult it is to love when the object of our love is weak and, to our earthly eyes, unlovely. As the months went by and Christopher continued to battle anxiety and doubt, I grew increasingly impatient and irritated. Rather than giving in to those feelings and pulling away from him—which I had been guilty of earlier in our marriage—I committed to draw near. Because I knew I would not succeed without help, my morning prayer became, "God, help me to love Christopher well today." That single prayer wasn't my only plan of action, but it did reorient me toward my husband.

Christopher also had to be forbearing in this season. When my insomnia kicked in after my father died, he had to endure my edginess and occasional despair as I functioned on far too little sleep. It takes a lot more effort and intentionality to love our spouse when they're not their best selves.

Every single marriage wrestles with variations on this theme. Will we choose to love lavishly when the scars are still raw from breast cancer surgery, when our spouse is in the grips of depression, or if they resist growing? I hope so because it's when we feel ugly or unworthy that we most need love. That's also when the consistent, sacrificial love that we offer our spouse can bring about the deepest healing.

The midlife crash course that Christopher and I went through taught us that we could not take our marriage for granted. I don't think any of us can. No marriage is invulnerable to failure, which means we all have to consistently show up and do the work. One essential component of that work involves imagining our future.

CREATING A UNIQUE MARRIAGE TELOS

Because God passed down his creative DNA to us and because the Holy Spirit dwells in us, we should be able to create and enjoy some of the best marriages on the planet. That won't happen by following formulas or emulating the plot line in our favorite movie. Instead, we have to partner with God to envision—or imagine—a future that's specific to our marriage. As that future starts to come into focus, we walk with our spouse, faithfully and resolutely, toward that goal. This becomes our marriage telos.

In chapter two, we talked about telos meaning the process of moving toward an end goal or a specific destination, as well as the overarching purpose that guides our lives. Because telos is dynamic and all-encompassing, figuring this out is not something we can do in an hour over the weekend. Our telos will emerge over time. And occasionally, it will require us to change our flight pattern. During this process, we want to be working toward a telos that is congruent with how God is and has been working in our lives.

As we attempt to discern our telos, a potential starting point might be to ask these two essential questions: "What are we aiming for, and how does each part of our lives contribute to this goal?" Our responses will depend on many variables, including our areas of gifting, our family's needs, our overall health, and our resources (e.g., finances, time, and energy). Every marriage, like every individual life, is meant to be oriented toward something.

The specific telos that we aim for and the way we move toward it should intertwine with our big-picture calling as Christians, which Jesus lays out in the Gospels:

> "You must love the LORD your God with all your heart, all your soul, and all your mind." This is the first and greatest commandment. A second is equally important: "Love your neighbor as yourself." The entire law and all the demands of the prophets are based on these two commandments. (Matthew 22:37-40)

By this point in life, we all know that wholeheartedly loving God and our neighbors (of which our spouse is the closest and most enduring) is no easy feat. Particularly if love *always* needs to be kind, patient, forgiving, hope-filled, and all those other descriptors found in Paul's infamous letter to the Corinthian church (1 Corinthians 13:4-7). Thankfully, God understands our limitations and our weaknesses. He knows sanctification does not happen overnight. We have our entire lives—our entire telos—to grow in our capacity to love. And it's an indication of God's abundant grace that it doesn't matter if you've been pursuing him for decades or if you just started last week. We're all invited to participate in this incredible story.

The love that we're growing into should draw us deeper into relationship with God and compel us to both worship him and bring his kingdom to earth. In other words, the vertical (heavenly) love transforms us, and then both motivates and enables us to love horizontally. That kingdom-building, horizontal love includes battling injustice, restoring the earth, feeding the hungry, changing diapers, forgiving our spouse, and massaging oil on our parent's feet. It's in the very process of loving and serving that our imaginations come alive and we can begin to dream about our unique marriage telos.

In the early stages of our relationship—when we were blissfully unaware of what the future would hold—most of us probably did a lot of dreaming. Before Christopher and I got married, we imagined what our first apartment might look like, where we would travel, and how often we'd have sex. Back then, our imaginations were mostly shaped by cultural norms, feel-good hormones, and unrealistic expectations. Because many of us have spent the last ten, twenty, or thirty years together, we can now imagine a marriage based on reality rather than fantasy.

Though some of us are more susceptible to magical thinking than others, we all need to recognize the difference between dreams and fantasies. Dreams help us to envision real possibilities because they are connected to our potential and our gifts. Fantasies funnel us into cul-de-sacs because they appeal to our pride and are largely based on others' strengths and capabilities. So dream big but stay grounded in God and in your reality.

As you dream, consider where you feel most engaged as a couple. Where are the two of you at your best: hosting dinner parties, praying for others, taking on household projects, coaching town soccer, or maybe volunteering at the local animal shelter?

The places where we feel most engaged partnering together are often the very places where our marriage is poised to uniquely serve the greater good. Remember, our telos isn't only about us. Yes, marriage will make us holy—assuming we let it—but that can't be the only or even the main goal. Holiness, or Christlikeness, should propel us to serve and bless others.

There are specific, unique objectives that you and your spouse will be able to accomplish better than anyone else. For example, Christopher and I are rather fearless in the emotional/relational realm. We're not phased about vulnerably sharing our lives with the world. Hence this book. However, because we're both somewhat terrified of power tools with sharp, spinning blades, we would not be good candidates for a Habitat for Humanity building project. (Unless they wanted us to offer marriage counseling during lunch breaks.) That kind of self-awareness puts helpful parameters on our imagination and prevents us from chasing after grandiose, unrealistic schemes.

It's also worth considering where the two of you have the most conflict or stress when you try to partner together. Whatever it may be, your strife does not necessarily indicate that you should avoid this activity. Perhaps this is the exact area where you need to dig in and grow. Christopher and I used to have consistent conflict when planning our vacations. Not going on vacation wasn't an option, so we worked on hearing each other's concerns and adjusting our expectations. We can now plan our vacations without fighting—provided that I honor his need to stay on budget and he honors my need to stay someplace beautiful.

If you're struggling to discern your marriage telos, go back to the earlier phases of your relationship: your stones of remembrance. How does your past want to inform your future? Almost twenty years ago Christopher and I led a Good Friday service in a local prison and both felt incredibly energized. We never forgot the experience, but kids and health issues forced us to put the idea of returning on hold. When our youngest son started applying to colleges and we could foresee our family dynamic shifting, we knew it was time. We now do a monthly service at a nearby correctional facility and truly love being with these men.

When our kids were young, we biked all over the city of Boston with them in tow. When we moved out of the city to the country, we swapped our bikes for a minivan. Recently, Christopher and I began imagining how we could exercise together, and upon recalling that earlier season, we decided to buy new bicycles. We're now rediscovering the joy of biking—provided we stay on the (flat) rail trails. Serving in the prison and biking are two very different components of our telos, but they both help us to stay connected and fulfill our calling.

Imagining our telos requires us to do a thorough inventory. Remember those midflight questions I brought up in chapter two? Ask them or something similar to them on a regular basis: Where are we in sync? Where are we out of sync, and how long has that been true? Where have we defaulted to autopilot, and how is that choice affecting us? In this honest space we can course correct or begin to create something new and authentic.

No two people are identical, which means every marriage and every marriage telos will be different. When planning for our future, it's wise to consider if we're "writing our own biography, or xeroxing a script." Are we relying on "our own imaginative faculty, or have we let ourselves be hijacked by the clichés and propaganda with which we are continually bombarded?" Creating something original takes more work, but copying leads to comparison, frustration, and ultimately, wasting our talents.

As we face the various crises of midlife, remember, the role of the imagination is to bring hope, break through despair, solve problems, and energize us. The more intimate our relationship with God, the more comfortable we'll be trusting the Holy Spirit to guide our imaginative process.

CRISIS OR OPPORTUNITY?

This brings us back to my original question: Is midlife marriage a crisis or an opportunity? It's both. Without a doubt, midlife will shake us to the core. Repeatedly. We will feel incompetent and over-whelmed on a regular basis. But we will also feel empowered and victorious as we overcome obstacles and learn how to do things we've never done before.

Every couple I interviewed faced the challenges and surprises of midlife head on, with their eyes and hearts wide open. They stayed engaged, exhibited resilience and malleability, and moved toward God and each other. They also refused to allow their failures to define them and instead grieved their losses and course corrected. They grew and changed—individually and as a couple. They believed that God really does take our ashes and transform them into something beautiful.

Though our losses might be compounding in quick succession, the horror of those losses won't stop the flow of blessings. It's also true that the richness of the blessings can't—and won't—diminish the pain of our loss. Embracing this paradox stretches our souls so they can contain all that God is doing in and through us.

Of this we can be assured: the God of the universe walks with us during seasons of sickness and health, abundance and lack, certainty and doubt, always offering us the hope of glory. He empowers us to love well, forgive fully, and spend whatever days we have left making our marriages, our families, and our communities increasingly beautiful.

I'd like to leave you with the benediction from Jude that a friend sang at the conclusion of our wedding ceremony:

To him who is able to keep you from stumbling and to present you before his glorious presence without fault and with great joy—to the only God our Savior be glory, majesty, power and authority, through Jesus Christ our Lord, before all ages, now and forevermore! (Jude 24-25 NIV)

Amen and amen.

GOING DEEPER

1. Consider Janine Langan's question: "When planning our future, are we writing our own biography, or xeroxing a script?" How might God be asking you to discard someone else's script and write your own? Be specific.

2. If there are any places in your marriage where you feel stuck or have lost energy, how could you reengage? Over the course of the next year, consider asking God to help you hope and dream for change. What might that change look like? (If you are at a loss of what to talk about, consider listening to a podcast together, perhaps over dinner, and then discussing the content.)

3. How is God calling you to love and serve your spouse and your family? Again, be specific. What spiritual work do you need to do to make that happen?

4. What are you and your spouse currently doing to serve your community or the larger needs of the world? If there's no space or time in the current season to start anything new, consider asking God to reveal what the next season might hold.

ACKNOWLEDGMENTS

For the women and men who bravely, humbly shared your lives, thank you for your honesty and courage. Your stories have made this book so much richer.

Hannah Anderson: I am so grateful for your partnership, your scholarly mind, and your pastor's heart. This book would not be what it is without your input and support.

A huge thanks to my early readers, editors, advisers, and chocolate suppliers: Christopher Greco, Sheila and Nick Rowe, Dr. Emily Polis Gibson, Jen Pollock Michel, Dr. John Peteet, Wendy Alsup, Mardi D'Olfo Smith, Garrett and Nici Smith, John Reichart, Kim Findlay, Kristen Johnson, Dr. Jeffrey Bjorck, Dr. Susan Buckner, Ezer Kang, Ashley Hales, Virginia Freisen, Paul Goodwin-Groen, Tess Pope, Danny Tao, Carlene Hill Byron, Amy Simpson, Kim Harms, Stephanie Allen Reeves, Anna Moseley Gissing, Rebecca and Joel Russell, Brad Wong, Lisa Washington Lamb, Ray Kollbocker, Carolyn Parr, Jo-Hannah Reardon, Linda Kerr MacKillop, Margot Starbuck, Raquel Menezes, Kara Wetzel, Shawn Healy, Marya Lowry, Capt. Andrew Linton, Diana Batarseh, John and Amber Carroll, Kimberly Knight, Rachel Wilson, and Gerald and Laurie Walle. If you gave me input and I've forgotten to list you, please forgive me!

To my Patreon team: Drs. Val and Tom Andrews, Beth and David Frawley, Kimberly and Alex Knight, Dan and Kathy Szatkowski, Peter and Stephanie Choo, Barbara Brescia, Kathy and Gary MacDonald, Jeff and Sharon Bjorck, Rachel Wilson, Alistair and Rebecca Bell, Chelsea and Peter Vessenes, Lisa Calderon, Marc and Serena Hildenbrand, Deidre and Danny Tao, Karen Stevenson,

Jessica Finch, Sheila and Nick Rowe, Sonia and Gabe Andreson, Sincy Varghese, and Gretchen Saalbach. Thank you for believing in me.

Thank you to the many authors and theologians who challenge my thinking and shape my writing, including Beth Felker Jones, Carolyn Custis James, Karen Swallow Prior, Jonathan Grant, Andy Crouch, Alice Mathews, LaTasha Morrison, and Mike Mason.

To the librarians at Reuben Hoar Library, thank you for constantly extending my due dates and serving me with a smile.

To Sean and Laura Richmond, thank you for your prayers, your friendship, and for providing us with a safe place to land.

The generous, talented crew at IVP: Ethan McCarthy, thanks for grabbing this proposal when it came across your desk; Elissa Schauer, thank you for taking the baton from Ethan, pushing me to find my own words, and exhibiting patience with my slow process; Lori Neff, Tara Burns, Krista Clayton, Allison Noble, and Rebecca Gill, I am indebted to you for helping readers discover this book; and special thanks to the design team for making the book both elegant and readable.

Thanks to my agent, Karen Neumair, at Credo Communications, for knowing where to place this curious project.

Special thanks to the brilliant women of Redbud Writers Guild and the Pelican Project.

To Mom and Charles: thank you for your ongoing love and support of our crazy family. To my sisters, Leslie and Jane: I love and appreciate you both—more with each passing year. To Christopher, my love: Let's do everything in our power to make the next twenty-nine years richer, deeper, and even more meaningful. Much love and gratitude to our three sons and two daughters-in-law: Anthony and Kate, GianCarlo and Charlotte, and Matthew. Papa and I hope that the work we've done in our own marriage will bless all of you for years to come.

To the God who thought of me, breathed life into me, and continues to sustain me, thank you.

ADDITIONAL RESOURCES

Please note: Listing these books does not necessarily mean that I wholeheartedly agree with the authors' points of view. Read with discernment.

AGING AND MIDLIFE

Bradley Hagerty, Barbara. *Life Reimagined: The Science, Art, and Opportunity of Midlife*. New York: Riverhead Books, 2017.

Gawande, Atul. *Being Mortal: Illness, Medicine, and What Matters in the End*. New York: Profile Books, 2014.

Gross, Jane. *A Bitter Sweet Season: Caring for Our Aging Parents—and Ourselves*. New York: Knopf, 2011.

Palmer, Parker J. *On the Brink of Everything: Grace, Gravity, and Getting Old*. Oakland, CA: Berrett-Koehler, 2018.

Rauch, Jonathan. *The Happiness Curve: Why Life Gets Better After 50*. New York: Thomas Dunne, 2018.

Van Loon, Michelle. *Becoming Sage: Cultivating Meaning, Purpose, and Spirituality in Midlife*. Chicago: Moody Publishers, 2020.

FAITH, SPIRITUALITY, AND TRANSFORMATION

Allender, Dan B. *The Healing Path: How the Hurts in Your Past Can Lead You to a More Abundant Life*. Colorado Springs, CO: WaterBrook Press, 1999.

Anderson, Hannah. *All That's Good: Recovering the Lost Art of Discernment*. Chicago: Moody Press, 2018.

Brueggeman, Walter. *The Prophetic Imagination*. Minneapolis: Augsburg Fortress, 2001.

Cloud, Henry, and John Townsend. *How People Grow: What the Bible Reveals About Personal Growth*. Grand Rapids, MI: Zondervan, 2001.

Graves, Marlena. *Beautiful Disaster: Finding Hope in the Midst of Brokenness*. Grand Rapids, MI: Brazos, 2014.

Leyland Fields, Leslie. *Forgiving Our Fathers and Mothers*. Nashville: Thomas Nelson, 2014.

Nouwen, Henri J. M. *The Inner Voice of Love: A Journey Through Anguish to Freedom*. New York: Image Books, 1998.

Peterson, Eugene. *A Long Obedience in the Same Direction: Discipleship in an Instant Society*. Downers Grove, IL: InterVarsity Press, 2019.

Pollock Michel, Jen. *Teach Us to Want: Longing, Ambition, and the Life of Faith*. Downers Grove, IL: InterVarsity Press, 2014.

Ryken, Leland, ed. *The Christian Imagination: The Practice of Faith in Literature and Writing*. Colorado Springs, CO: WaterBrook Press, 2002.

Saxton, Jo. *The Dream of You: Let Go of Broken Identities and Live the Life You Were Made For*. Colorado Springs, CO: WaterBrook, 2018.

Smith, Gordon T. *Called to Be Saints: An Invitation to Christian Maturity*. Downers Grove, IL: InterVarsity Press, 2013.

Smith, James Bryan. *The Good and Beautiful Life: Putting on the Character of Christ*. Downers Grove, IL: InterVarsity Press, 2009.

Wright, Nicholas Thomas. *After You Believe: Why Christian Character Matters*. New York: HarperOne, 2012.

HEALTH ISSUES, SELF-CARE, AND TRAUMA

Herman, Judith, M.D., *Trauma and Recovery: The Aftermath of Violence—from Domestic Abuse to Political Terror*. New York: Basic Books, 1992.

Nakazawa, Donna Jackson. *Childhood Disrupted: How Your Biography Becomes Your Biology, and How You Can Heal*. New York: Atria Books, 2016.

Simpson, Amy. *Anxious: Choosing Faith in a World of Worry*. Downers Grove, IL: InterVarsity Press, 2014.

van der Kolk, Bessel, *The Body Keeps the Score: Brain, Mind, and Body in the Healing of Trauma*. New York: Viking, 2014.

Yamasaki, April. *Four Gifts: Seeking Self-Care for Heart, Soul, Mind, and Strength*. Harrisonburg, VA: Herald Press, 2018.

LOSS AND GRIEF

Bowler, Kate. *Everything Happens for a Reason: And Other Lies I've Loved*. New York: Random House, 2018.

Didion, Joan. *The Year of Magical Thinking*. New York: Knopf, 2005.

Kalanithi, Paul. *When Breath Becomes Air*. New York: Random House, 2016.

Lewis, C. S. *The Problem of Pain*. Rev. ed. New York: HarperOne, 2015.

Rah, Soong-Chan. *Prophetic Lament: A Call for Justice in Troubled Times*. Downers Grove, IL: InterVarsity Press, 2015.

Sampson, Aubrey. *The Louder Song: Listening for Hope in the Midst of Lament*. Colorado Springs, CO: NavPress, 2019.

Sandberg, Sheryl, and Adam Grant. *Option B: Facing Adversity, Building Resilience, and Finding Joy*. New York: Knopf, 2017.

Sittser, Jerry. *A Grace Disguised: How the Soul Grows through Loss*. Grand Rapids, MI: Zondervan, 2004.

MARRIAGE, PARENTING, AND FAMILY

Cheng-Tozun, Dorcas. *Start, Love, Repeat: How to Stay in Love with Your Entrepreneur in a Crazy Start-Up World*. New York: Center Street, 2017.

Crouch, Andy. *The Tech-Wise Family: Everyday Steps for Putting Technology in Its Proper Place*. Grand Rapids, MI: Baker, 2017.

Greco, Dorothy Littell. *Making Marriage Beautiful: Lifelong Love, Joy, and Intimacy Start with You*. Colorado Springs, CO: David C. Cook, 2017.

Johnson, Sue. *Hold Me Tight: Seven Conversations for a Lifetime of Love*. New York: Little, Brown Spark, 2008.

Karen, Robert. *Becoming Attached: First Relationships and How They Shape Our Capacity to Love*. New York: Oxford University Press, 1998.

Mason, Mike. *The Mystery of Marriage: Meditations on the Miracle*. Colorado Springs, CO: Multnomah Press, 2005.

McNiel, Catherine. *Long Days of Small Things: Motherhood as a Spiritual Discipline*. Colorado Springs, CO: NavPress, 2017.

Tripp, Paul David. *What Did You Expect? Redeeming the Realities of Marriage*. Wheaton, IL: Crossway, 2015.

SEX AND SEXUALITY

Allender, Dan B. *The Wounded Heart: Hope for Adult Victims of Sexual Abuse*. Colorado Springs, CO: NavPress, 1990.

Comiskey, Andrew. *Strength in Weakness: Healing Sexual and Relational Brokenness*. Downers Grove, IL: InterVarsity Press, 2003.

Felker Jones, Beth. *Faithful: A Theology of Sex*. Grand Rapids, MI: Zondervan, 2015.

Grant, Jonathan. *Divine Sex: A Compelling Vision for Christian Relationships in a Hypersexualized Age.* Grand Rapids, MI: Brazos, 2015.

Hiestand, Gerald, and Todd Wilson. *Beauty, Order, and Mystery: A Christian Vision of Human Sexuality.* Downers Grove, IL: InterVarsity Press, 2017.

Stringer, Jay. *Unwanted: How Sexual Brokenness Reveals Our Way to Healing.* Colorado Springs, CO: NavPress, 2018.

West, Christopher. *Theology of the Body for Beginners: A Basic Introduction to Pope John Paul's II's Sexual Revolution.* West Chester, PA, Ascension Press, 2004.

WEBSITES

EMDR Therapy: www.emdr.com

The Trauma Center website: www.traumacenter.org

The Center for Disease Control Adverse Childhood Experiences website and test: www.cdc.gov/violenceprevention/childabuseandneglect/acestudy/about.html

National Domestic Abuse Hotline: https://www.thehotline.org/is-this-abuse/abuse-defined/

NOTES

1 THE PARADOX OF MIDLIFE MARRIAGE

8   *This is a time when you shift gears*: Barbara Bradley Hagerty, *Life Reimagined: The Science, Art, and Opportunity of Midlife* (New York: Riverhead Books: 2017), 5.

a portal for expanding our souls: Mary Pipher, *Women Rowing North: Navigating Life's Currents and Flourishing as We Age* (New York: Bloomsbury Publishing, 2019), 17, 20.

9   *the strength and speed of our response*: Sheryl Sandberg and Adam Grant, *Option B: Facing Adversity, Building Resilience, and Finding Joy* (New York: Knopf, 2017), 10.

2 TELOS

14   *We engage our memories*: Casey Tygrett, *As I Recall: Discovering the Place of Memories in Our Spiritual Life* (Downers Grove, IL: InterVarsity Press, 2019), 12.

16   *stone of remembrance*: Michelle Van Loon, *Moments and Days: How Our Holy Celebrations Shape Our Faith* (Colorado Springs, CO: NavPress, 2016), 89.

being fundamentally changed: Ruth Haley Barton, *Life Together in Christ: Experiencing Transformation in Community* (Downers Grove, IL: InterVarsity Press; 2014), 11.

20   *Having sex outside of marriage*: Sexual idolatry is not simply having sex outside of a covenanted marriage. It can happen within a marriage if one or both spouses fails to understand or practice sexual intimacy as God intended. This will be discussed more fully in chapters 7 and 8.

21   *the "tiny parasite" called greed*: Eugene H. Peterson, *Tell It Slant* (Grand Rapids, MI: Eerdmans, 2008), 62.

22   *a process that includes deciding together*: Hannah Anderson, email exchange with the author, December 5, 2019.

telos is that it's "a guiding purpose": Jonathan Grant, *Divine Sex: A Compelling Vision for Christian Relationships in a Hypersexualized Age* (Grand Rapids, MI: Brazos, 2015), 119.

23   *fasten their seat belts*: Personal correspondence with Capt. Andrew Linton.

We who believe: Luci Shaw, "Beauty and the Creative Impulse," in *The Christian Imagination: the Practice of Faith in Literature and Writing*, ed. Leland Ryken (Colorado Springs, CO: Shaw Books, 2002), 94.

24   *an act of hope*: Janine Langan, "The Christian Imagination," in *Christian Imagination*, 65.

The task of the prophetic imagination: Walter Brueggemann, *The Prophetic Imagination* (Minneapolis, Fortress Press), 63.

29   *if we keep the first commandment*: Eugene H. Peterson, *Tell It Slant* (Grand Rapids, MI: Eerdmans, 2008), 63.

3 CH, CH, CH, CHANGES

32   *hormones carry "messages to and from all organs"*: Elizabeth Lee Vliet, MD, *Screaming to Be Heard: Hormonal Connections Women Suspect . . . and Doctors Still Ignore* (Lanham, MD: Rowman & Littlefield, 2005), 25.

33   *It is very common for women*: Christine Northrup, *The Wisdom of Menopause: Creating Physical and Emotional Health and Healing During the Change* (New York: Random House, 2012), 53.

34   *only 59 percent of Americans*: Jeffrey M. Jones, "In U.S., 40% Get Less Than Recommended Amount of Sleep," Gallup News, December 19, 2013, https://news.gallup.com/poll/166553/less-recommended-amount-sleep.aspx.

     nearly half of all women: Anjel Vahratian, "Sleep Duration and Quality Among Women Aged 40-59, by Menopausal Status," Centers for Disease Control and Prevention, September 2017, www.cdc.gov/nchs/products/databriefs/db286.htm.

35   *cognitive impairment, heart issues*: "Sleep Deprivation and Deficiency," U.S. Department of Health & Human Services, www.nhlbi.nih.gov/health-topics/sleep-deprivation-and-deficiency.

     one in ten Americans battles: "NIH Analysis Shows Americans Are in Pain," National Center for Complementary and Integrative Health, August 11, 2015, https://nccih.nih.gov/news/press/08112015.

36   *likelihood of contracting cancer*: "Diet and Physical Activity: What's the Cancer Connection?" American Cancer Society, www.cancer.org/cancer/cancer-causes/diet-physical-activity/diet-and-physical-activity.html.

37   *What would it mean for Christians*: Kate Bowler, *Everything Happens for a Reason: And Other Lies I've Loved* (New York: Random House, 2018), 21.

38   *highest rates of depression*: Laura A. Pratt and Debra J. Brody, "Depression in the U.S. Household Population, 2009-2012," Centers for Disease Control and Prevention, December 2014, www.cdc.gov/nchs/products/databriefs/db172.htm.

     All mental illness, by definition: Amy Simpson, *Troubled Minds: Mental Illness and the Church's Mission* (Downers Grove, IL: InterVarsity Press, 2013), 34.

     In those first months: Alia Joy, "When I Am Bipolar," *The Mudroom* (blog), May 10, 2017, http://mudroomblog.com/when-i-am-bipolar.

     fear is a response: Amy Simpson, *Anxious: Choosing Faith in a World of Worry* (Downers Grove, IL: InterVarsity Press, 2014), 21.

39   *victorious Christian living*: Simpson, *Troubled Minds*, 104.

41   *a don't-do list*: April Yamasaki, *Four Gifts: Seeking Self-Care for Heart, Soul, Mind, and Strength* (Harrisonburg, VA: Herald Press, 2018), 45.

4 PULLED IN TWO—OR MORE—DIRECTIONS

49   *started our families a bit later in life*: The mean age for becoming a mother is now slightly over twenty-six and the current age for first-time marriage is twenty-eight for men and twenty-six for women. See T. J. Mathews and Brady E. Hamilton, "Mean Age of Mothers Is on the Rise," NCHS Data Brief, January 2016, www.cdc.gov/nchs/data/databriefs/db232.pdf; and D'Vera Cohn, Jeffrey S. Passel, Wendy Wang, and Gretchen Livingston, "Barely Half of U.S. Adults Are Married—A Record Low," Pew Research Center, December 14, 2011, www.pewsocialtrends.org/2011/12/14/barely-half-of-u-s-adults-are-married-a-record-low.

51   *to successfully launch our kids*: This might not be the case if you have a child who has special needs or who requires long-term care.

52   *Never before*: Jane Gross, *A Bittersweet Season: Caring for Our Aging Parents—And Ourselves* (New York: Vintage Books, 2012), 4.

53   *Pew Research Center*: Kim Parker and Eileen Patten, "Emotional Ties," Pew Research Center, January 30, 2013, www.pewsocialtrends.org/2013/01/30/emotional-ties.

53   *average monthly Social Security payment*: "As They Near Retirement, Baby Boomers Remain Unprepared," Insured Retirement Institute, April 10, 2018, www.myirionline .org/newsroom/newsroom-detail-view/as-they-near-retirement-baby-boomers -remain-unprepared.

      During the last week of his treatments: These events are also explored in Dorothy Littell Greco, "How to Stay Married When You're Stuck Between Needy Teens and Aging Parents," *Christianity Today*, accessed February 11, 2020, www.christianitytoday.com/women/2018 /october/divorce-marriage-midlife-stuck-between-needy-teens-aging-pa.html.

55   *In our parents' greatest hour*: Leslie Leyland Fields, *Forgiving Our Fathers and Mothers: Finding Freedom from Hurt and Hate* (Nashville: W Publishing, 2014), 138.

56   *bump in the divorce rate*: Susan L. Brown, I-Fen Lin, and Krista K. Payne, "Age Variation in Divorce Rate, 1990-2012," National Center for Family and Marriage Research, www .bgsu.edu/content/dam/BGSU/college-of-arts-and-sciences/NCFMR/documents/FP /FP-12-05.pdf, accessed February 11, 2020.

58   *one-downmanship*: Mike Mason, *The Mystery of Marriage: Meditations on the Miracle* (Colorado Springs, CO: Multnomah Press, 2005), 151.

6 NAVIGATING TRAUMA AND LOSS

78   *Katherine and Rick received a frantic phone call*: Katherine James shares more of their story in *A Prayer for Orion: A Son's Addiction and a Mother's Love* (Downers Grove, IL: InterVarsity Press, 2020).

79   *traumatic events generally involve*: Judith Herman, M.D., *Trauma and Recovery: The Aftermath of Violence—From Domestic Abuse to Political Terror* (New York: Basic Books, 1997), 33.

      Statistics show: Bessel van der Kolk, *The Body Keeps the Score: Brain, Mind, and Body in the Healing of Trauma* (New York: Viking Press, 2014), 1; and "Statistics," National Sexual Violence Resource Center, www.nsvrc.org/node/4737, accessed February 11, 2020.

80   *anyone over the age of fifty who experienced*: Herman, *Trauma and Recovery*: chapters 1 and 6.

81   *depression, cardiovascular disease, and autoimmune diseases*: "Past Trauma May Haunt Your Future Health," *Harvard Women's Health Watch*, February 2019, www.health .harvard.edu/diseases-and-conditions/past-trauma-may-haunt-your-future-health.

82   *eye movement desensitization and reprocessing*: This is known as EMDR. See resource section for more on this type of therapy as well as a link for the Adverse Childhood Experiences test.

      In fact, intimate relationships: Herman, *Trauma and Recovery*, chapters 3 and 7.

      troubles start to cluster at midlife: Barbara Bradley Hagerty, *Life Reimagined: The Science, Art, and Opportunity of Midlife* (New York: Riverhead Books, 2017), 235.

83   *passed our expiration date*: Hagerty, *Life Reimagined*, 331.

85   *Approximately ten million men and women*: M. C. Black et al., "National Intimate Partner and Sexual Violence Survey," Centers for Disease Control and Prevention, November 2011, www.cdc.gov/violenceprevention/pdf/nisvs_report2010-a.pdf.

      When physical violence follows: It's beyond the scope of this book to adequately address marital abuse. Please see the appendix for more resources and reach out for help if this is an issue in your marriage.

86   *If I ever become a saint*: Mother Teresa, *Mother Teresa: Come Be My Light* (New York: Doubleday Religion, 2009), 230.

87   *God uses the desert of the soul*: Marlena Graves, *Beautiful Disaster: Finding Hope in the Midst of Brokenness* (Grand Rapids, MI: Brazos, 2014), 6.

88   *the promise of* and *in an either-or world*: Jen Pollock Michel, *Surprised by Paradox: The Promise of* And *in an Either-Or World* (Downers Grove, IL: InterVarsity Press, 2019), chap. 1.

89   *no change takes place in marriage*: Paul David Tripp, *What Did You Expect? Redeeming the Realities of Marriage* (Wheaton, IL: Crossway, 2015), 72.

91   *Empathy begins with listening deeply*: April Yamaski, email correspondence with the author, January 17, 2018.

92   *I am a great coward*: C. S. Lewis, *The Problem of Pain*, rev. ed. (New York: HarperOne, 2015), 104-5.

7 CREATED TO CONNECT

98   *bonding is the ability to establish*: Henry Cloud, *Changes That Heal: How to Understand the Past to Ensure a Healthier Future* (Grand Rapids, MI: Zondervan, 1990), 61.

   attachment theory: See more on attachment theory and marriage in Dorothy Littell Greco, "Your Childhood Wounds May Be Hurting Your Marriage," *Christianity Today*, January 24, 2018, www.christianitytoday.com/women/2018/january/your-childhood-wounds-may-be-hurting-your-marriage.html.

99   *Without a secure base established in infancy*: Marshall Klaus, John Kennell, and Phyllis Klaus, *Bonding: Building the Foundations of Secure Attachment and Independence* (Reading, MA: Addison Wesley, 1995), 192.

99   *Relationship, or bonding*: Cloud, *Changes That Heal*, 65.

100 *ezer kenegdo, or warrior ally for Adam*: Carolyn Custis James, *Half the Church: Recapturing God's Global Vision for Women* (Grand Rapids, MI: Zondervan, 2010), chap. 5.

   emotional umbilical cord: Klaus, Kennell, and Klaus, *Bonding*, chap. 9.

101 *ongoing responses between a mother and child*: Father and other consistent caregivers are also crucial during this time. Most research studies have focused on the mother-child relationship, which means there's less information about how other early relationships affect children. This does not discredit Bowlby's or other researchers' work, but it does balance out the emphasis on mother-child relationship.

   the "longer partners feel disconnected": Sue Johnson, *Hold Me Tight: Seven Conversations for a Lifetime of Love* (London: Little, Brown Spark, 2008), 31.

   one forms images of the self: Robert Karen, *Becoming Attached: First Relationships and How They Shape Our Capacity to Love* (New York: Oxford University Press, 1998), 202. See also Mary D. Salter Ainsworth, et al., *Patterns of Attachment* (New York: Psychology Press, 2015).

102 *Avoidantly attached adults*: Rachel Heller and Amir Levine, *Attached: The New Science of Adult Attachment and How It Can Help You Find—and Keep—Love* (New York: Tarcher, 2010), 93.

103 *primary fears of all human beings*: Bowlby in Klaus, Kennel, and Klaus, *Bonding*, 197.

104 *when we perceive a negative shift*: Johnson, *Hold Me Tight*, 35-36.

   security, or the lack of it: Klaus, Kennell, and Klaus, *Bonding*, 191-92.

105 *After you have experienced something*: Bessel van der Kolk, *The Body Keeps the Score: Brain, Mind, and Body in the Healing of Trauma* (New York: Penguin, 2014), 13.

106   *all relationships require translation*: Suzanne Stabile, *The Path Between Us: An Enneagram Journey to Healthy Relationships* (Downers Grove, IL: InterVarsity Press, 2018), 3.

108   *67 percent of adults*: Gretchen Livingston, "The Demographics of Remarriage," Pew Research Center, November 14, 2014, www.pewsocialtrends.org/2014/11/14 /chapter-2-the-demographics-of-remarriage.

109   *The trauma of losing our first marriages*: Diana Batarseh, personal correspondence with the author, January 8, 2020.

8 SEX, PART 1

119   *Evil hates the beauty of sex*: Jay Stringer, *Unwanted: How Sexual Brokenness Reveals Our Way to Healing* (Colorado Springs, CO: NavPress, 2018), 4.

   We serve a God who asks: Here and throughout chapters 8 and 9 I am indebted to the work of Beth Felker Jones, particularly her book *Faithful: A Theology of Sex* (Grand Rapids, MI: Zondervan, 2015), chap. 1.

121   *Beth Felker Jones states*: Jones, *Faithful*, 24.

122   *The Gospel is meant to*: Christopher West, *The Theology of the Body for Beginners: Rediscovering the Meaning of Life, Love, Sex, and Gender* (North Palm Beach, FL: Beacon, 2018), 39.

125   *80-90% of men view sex*: Juli Slattery, "Understanding Your Husband's Sexual Needs," *Focus on the Family*, January 1, 2009, www.focusonthefamily.com/marriage/sex-and -intimacy/understanding-your-husbands-sexual-needs/understanding-your-husbands -sexual-needs.

126   *Twenty percent of men admit*: "The Stats on Internet Pornography," OnlineSchools, accessed February 12, 2020, www.techaddiction.ca/files/porn-addiction-statistics.jpg.

127   *Repeated exposure to pornography*: William M. Struthers, *Wired for Intimacy: How Pornography Hijacks the Male Brain* (Downers Grove, IL: InterVarsity Press, 2009), 85.

   pornography portrays men and women: William M. Struthers, "The Effects of Porn on the Male Brain," *Christian Research Journal*, February 1, 2013, www.equip.org/article/the -effects-of-porn-on-the-male-brain-3.

   Using pornography and masturbating: Jonathan Grant, *Divine Sex: A Compelling Vision for Christian Relationships in a Hypersexualized Age* (Grand Rapids, MI: Brazos, 2015), 175.

128   *a feeling that we do not measure up*: Lewis B. Smedes, *Shame and Grace: Healing the Shame We Don't Deserve* (Grand Rapids, MI: Zondervan 1993), 5-6.

129   *one of the most fundamental*: Mike Mason, *The Mystery of Marriage: Meditations on the Miracle* (Colorado Springs, CO: Multnomah Press, 2005), 131.

132   *Our sexuality is indeed a powerful*: Debra Hirsch, *Redeeming Sex: Naked Conversations about Sex and Sexuality* (Downers Grove, IL, InterVarsity Press, 2015), 31.

9 SEX, PART 2

135   *Of all the things God has created*: Juli Slattery, *Rethinking Sexuality: God's Design and Why It Matters* (Colorado Springs, CO: Multnomah, 2018), 53.

137   *Making love is creating unity*: Tara M. Owens, *Embracing the Body: Finding God in Our Flesh and Bone* (Downers Grove, IL: InterVarsity Press, 2015), 212-13.

137   *Drawing upon the ancient marriage formula*: Gerald Hiestand, "Put Pain Like That Beyond My Power," in *Beauty, Order, and Mystery: A Christian Vision of Human Sexuality*, ed. Gerald Hiestand and Todd Wilson (Downers Grove, IL: InterVarsity Press, 2017), 111.

142   *To be naked with another person*: Mike Mason, *The Mystery of Marriage: Meditations on the Miracle* (Colorado Springs, CO: Multnomah Press, 2005), 129.

143   *our yes!*: Christopher West, *The Theology of the Body for Beginners* (North Palm Beach, FL: Beacon, 2018), 94.

145   *Sex is one of those mysteries*: Mason, *The Mystery of Marriage*, 139.

10 COMMUNITY

154   *accountability is "proactive honesty"*: Brad Wong, email exchange with the author, March 23, 2018.

155   *accountability can be an external pressure*: Wong, email exchange.

159   *make it count*: Dorothy Littell Greco, *Making Marriage Beautiful: Lifelong Love, Joy, and Intimacy Start with You* (Colorado Springs, CO: David C. Cook, 2017), 161.

     They didn't try to fix it: Kim Findlay, interview with author, January 29, 2019.

     I would've loved for them: Findlay.

     lament is a cry of injustice: Alia Joy, *Glorious Weakness: Discovering God in All We Lack* (Grand Rapids, MI: Baker, 2019), 155-56.

160   *Lament can lead us back*: Aubrey Sampson, *The Louder Song: Listening for Hope in the Midst of Lament* (Colorado Springs, CO: NavPress, 2019), 14.

     loneliness takes a physical toll: Janet Adamy and Paul Overberg, "The Loneliest Generation: Americans, More Than Ever, Are Aging Alone," *Wall Street Journal*, December 11, 2018, www.wsj.com/articles/the-loneliest-generation-americans-more-than-ever-are-aging-alone-11544541134?mod=e2fb.

161   *The people who were*: Robert Waldinger, "What Makes a Good Life? Lessons from the Longest Study on Happiness," *YouTube*, January 25, 2016, www.youtube.com/watch?v=8KkKuTCFvzI; and Liz Mineo, "Good Genes Are Nice, but Joy Is Better," *Harvard Gazette*, April 11, 2017, https://news.harvard.edu/gazette/story/2017/04/over-nearly-80-years-harvard-study-has-been-showing-how-to-live-a-healthy-and-happy-life.

166   *The hope of the gospel*: Jonathan Grant, *Divine Sex: A Compelling Vision for Christian Relationships in a Hypersexualized Age* (Grand Rapids, MI: Brazos, 2015), 53.

11 TELOS REPRISED

171   *What are we aiming for*: Jonathan Grant, *Divine Sex: A Compelling Vision for Christian Relationships in a Hypersexualized Age* (Grand Rapids, MI: Brazos, 2015), 142.

172   *Fantasies funnel us into cul-de-sacs*: Carlo Strenger and Arie Ruttenberg, "The Existential Necessity of Midlife Change," *Harvard Business Review*, February 2008, https://hbr.org/2008/02/the-existential-necessity-of-midlife-change.

174   *writing our own biography*: Janine Langan, "The Christian Imagination," in *The Christian Imagination*, ed. Leland Ryken (Colorado Springs, CO: Shaw Books, 2002), 72.

176   *consider listening to a podcast*: This suggestion comes courtesy of Jill Kandel while speaking at The Wonder Years Gathering, Feb. 23, 2020, Mt. Herman, CA.

ABOUT THE AUTHOR

Dorothy Littell Greco is a writer, speaker, marriage coach, and professional photographer who lives outside Boston. The author of *Making Marriage Beautiful*, Dorothy and her husband, Christopher, lead marriage workshops and retreats, speak at conferences nationwide, and have been helping couples create and sustain healthy marriages for more than twenty-five years.

Dorothy has written for *Christianity Today*, *Relevant Magazine*, *Missio Alliance*, MOPS, *Propel Women*, *Christians for Biblical Equality*, *The Perennial Gen*, Biola Center for Marriage and Family, and many other publications. She is a member of Redbud Writers Guild and The Pelican Project.

When she's not working, Dorothy loves to discuss theology, go for long walks and slow kayaks with Christopher, and share meals with friends.

You can connect with Dorothy and find more of her work on her website or by following her on social media:

website: www.dorothygreco.com
Instagram: @dorothylgreco
Facebook: Words&ImagesbyDorothyGreco
Twitter: @DorothyGreco